A Pattern of Herbs

by Meg Rutherford

A Pattern of Herbs

The Beautiful Island

Illustrated by Meg Rutherford

The Vegetable Book
by Yann Lovelock

A PATTERN OF HERBS

Herbs for goodness, food and health and how to identify and grow them

Written and illustrated by
MEG RUTHERFORD

With medical notes by
Ann Warren-Davis
Member of the National Institute of Medical Herbalists

Foreword by
F. Fletcher Hyde
Past President of the National Institute of Medical Herbalists

Dolphin Books
Doubleday & Company, Inc.
Garden City, New York
1976

Library of Congress Cataloging in Publication Data

Rutherford, Meg.
A pattern of herbs.

Bibliography: p. 154.
1. Herbs—Identification.   2. Herb gardening.
3. Cookery (Herbs).   4. Botany, Medical.
5. Materia medica, Vegetable.   I. Title.
SB351.H5R87   641.3'5'7
ISBN 0-385-07065-9
Library of Congress Catalog Card Number 74–18848

Acknowledgements

One cannot acknowledge fully all one's helpers, when an interest has been growing over so many years, and plants have been gathered over such a time and from so many friends, but I would like to offer my thanks to the following people. In particular Ann Warren-Davis, Consultant at the London Herbal Treatment Centre, to whom I am most indebted not only for my restored health but also for kindly giving up so much of her limited spare time for questions and advice, and for providing the sections on Herbal Medicine and the Medicinal properties and actions of the herbs.

I am very grateful to Mr. W. G. MacKenzie, who during his last year as Curator of the Chelsea Physic Garden was kind enough to let me use that lush and sun-warmed shelter for drawings and research, and found time to talk of Hemlock, and smaller, simpler plants. Also to Mr. and Mrs. Evetts of Ashfields Herb Nursery, Hinstock, Market Drayton, Shropshire, who supplied so many excellent plants to add to my collection for the purposes of this book. And to Mr. Ross and Dr. Melderis for access to information within the Department of Botany in the Natural History Museum.

I am in debt also to the following, who have variously answered my questions and offered advice and introductions, provided me with plants or helped to search for them. Miss J..Hope, of the Society of Herbalists, Mr. Lanning Roper, Nigel and Shirley Tuckley, Dr. Humphrey Bowen, Mrs. Rosemary Blake, also Axel and Roslyn

Poignant who, all unknowing, helped to point me down this path so many years ago.

My very special thanks are for my husband, Amis Goldingham, who not only had the courage to offer up advice and share in strange experiments with herbal drinks and dinners but also somehow found the time to help me in my searches for plants and information and to read and comment on the manuscript; all this without apparent ill-effect either to our relationship or to his love of plants.

Lastly, the unknown author whose recipes I used throughout, from

The Lady's Companion, London 1753
"Containing Upwards of Three Thousand different Receipts in
every Kind of Cookery; and Those the best and
most fashionable: being Four Times
the Quantity of any Book
of this Sort."

Foreword

The world of plants never fails to provide man with a source of pleasure, of food, of warmth and of health. Ancient records and the herbals of our forefathers enshrine life-preserving facts in a casket of jewelled words. A book on herbs may be cold, technical and frugally illustrated or it may consist of pictures lightly held together by prose and taking the reader by the hand into the magic of the countryside. Such is *A Pattern of Herbs*.

It is a pleasure to enjoy the delicate drawings throughout the volume with their restful neo-Victorian flavour and to browse among the exciting culinary fields opened up within its pages. The action and uses of the herbs in the restoration of health is an added bonus to a book of delight.

F. Fletcher Hyde, B.Sc., F.N.I.M.H.
Past President of the National Institute of
Medical Herbalists, U.K.

CONTENTS

Index of Herbs

INTRODUCTION

Two extremes of thought are current about herbs. One is that an interest in them is yet another social whim, superficial but tantalising. The other is that serious involvement must include awful happenings with toads in the dead of night, at a certain phase of the moon.

The simple truth is that herbs are wild plants which take from the soil all manner of minerals, and are rich in oils and vitamins. Man has learned to use these to his advantage, and as he moved about the earth he carried these plants to new places, so we find Mediterranean flora growing in the wake of the Romans, and later in the Americas and other colonies. From these strange lands new plants were brought to Europe.

To the layman interest generally centres around the kitchen, following some vague traditional habits which were once based on good sense, or experimenting with taste, which can bring some delicious surprises. But how many of us are aware that the use of Mint sauce originated to help digest the fatty young lamb, and now that lambs are no longer fatty, we continue to use the sauce for pleasure? Herbs are nowadays just as necessary a part of our food intake as when they constituted the only available medicine, and it was sensible to eat the cure with the cause.

Only last century most people would have had a fair knowledge of plant uses and their characteristics, as they still do in some country districts and round the Mediterranean. Now we are only aware that the countryside is full of plants, some of which we can eat, and that herbs will grow in a window-box or garden. But we are not always able to recognise the different plants, whether they grow already in our gardens or along the hedgerow.

This book is for people who have difficulty in identifying herbs. It is a result of long hours of frustration I felt when leaning over a green and growing enigma, armed with several books and an acute longing that the plant would oblige me by becoming the name I so desperately hoped it was, despite odd missing features. Attempting to will some plant into being what it is not is one of the hopeless comforts of the totally ignorant non-botanist. In England, London's Kew Gardens have a wonderful array of wild plants including almost all in this book. They are carefully bedded down under family names, taking most of the headaches out of the search. But Kew is not on everyone's doorstep, particularly when the Atlantic intervenes. It is in sympathy with other people who may have had some of my own problems in identifying plants that I have tried to simplify the search by these drawings. They cannot attempt to tell the whole story, but they may make the start a little easier.

Identification can be very difficult for the beginner. So many Thymes and Mints, and which is which? Then Tarragon, Hyssop and Savory can look horribly alike. Not the least of the problems is that reference is either over-simplified so as to ignore the fact that there may be other plants similar to that under scrutiny, or that many authorities have differing opinions. This is quite apart from the fact that local names vary and may bear no relation to those in another area. In addition, flavour, fragrance . . . and poison . . . vary, as can colour, size and shape, according to locality and condition.

Thus all the herbs drawn here, with the exception of one Rose and some of the poisonous plants and two Mayweeds, which I did not attempt to grow, will be as they were in the soil in my garden, their situation in that soil, and the weather, all of which may make them marginally different from those in other places, though they compared well with similar plants in the Chelsea Physic Garden and Kew Gardens. But the structure will be similar as will the flower. And those, as well as the overall type of plant, are the main points for identity. I have deliberately omitted hairs and similar detail unless I have found them to be important distinguishing features for the uninitiated. This may well upset botanists, but too many tiny details are inclined to obscure shape, and printing methods may not manage the degree of clarity needed, even if I could. The number of hairs on a Foxglove leaf is prodigious, and would in my opinion be quite impossible to deal with. Hairs rarely cover a plant evenly, but are likely to be distributed in different ways on different areas. For example Borage is almost completely covered with what appears to be an even distribution, but on the upper surface of the leaves the hairs increase in number towards the edges. We all know that Stinging Nettles are covered with unfriendly looking hairs, which I have left out in order to show as clearly as possible the particular shape of the stem. Interiors of flowers change with pollination, making "accurate" drawings of stamens, etc. somewhat difficult; if they obscured an important silhouette I did not draw them at all. Plants are, in any case, undergoing a continuous cycle of change, so that there can never be an ideal time to draw them, particularly as evolution in shape can make lower leaves such as those on Borage and Foxglove and some umbelliferous plants rather different from those on top.

This book concentrates on a selection of herbs which can in the main be used for cooking, in drinks and medicinally, but omits all but medicinal details for three familiar favourites, Bay, Chives and Parsley. These are between pp. xxii and xxvii. The Mints cross-pollinate and occur in so many varieties, as do the Thymes and Sages, that I have simply tried to show some of the main types within the first two groups, and left the Common Sage to suffice for its varieties. As most of those included can be found in some variety growing in the wild, it has seemed important also to try to find points of identity for a poisonous few which could be mistaken for safe herbs. Comfrey and Borage when young have leaves somewhat similar to those of the poisonous Foxglove, so space is given to try to clarify the differences between them. One of the greatest problems has been with the Umbelliferae, of which there are more than two thousand species, though only a proportion of them grow in the British Isles or America. Hemlock is one of these, as is Fool's Parsley; these are described in the last section on p. 145, along with other doubtful plants, two of which are also illustrated. Skulls are drawn beside poisonous plants (though not to scale) and half skulls by those

which should be treated with caution. My only warning here . . .
be very sure of your herbs before you eat them.

Ann Warren-Davis, M.N.I.M.H., has contributed notes on Herbal
Medicine on p. xviii, and some medical aspects of the herbs where
relevant, but has been deliberately brief, as self-diagnosis is an unwise pursuit. Headaches may feel the same, for example, but have
different causes, so some will be eased by teas, sometimes, but not as
a matter of course. Herbal medicine works because a Medical Herbalist can select a number of herbs which work together rather like
an orchestra . . . prescribed for a particular person, with a particular complaint, in a particular set of circumstances. Put at its simplest,
Herbal Medicine quite literally feeds the patient until a balance is
restored.

My own adventure with herbs must be typical. First the need for
a change from those dreary student meals, which led to an increasing row of dried herbs which stood on a damp shelf in a paraffin-
perfumed London basement, where no fresh plant could be per-
suaded to survive. Then holidays in Spain, where Rosemary and
Thyme breathed blissful odours into the warm air of the bays and
hillsides, and I thought wistfully of the faded souls which lay in
those small glass jars at home. Eventually, in a garden out of London, my own delicious clear fresh Mint grew wild among the grass.

Since then I have grown from seed, and muddled the seedlings,
so I grew them in chimney pots for clarity, incidentally making an
interchangeable garden and a control for mints. Other herbs have
been grown from cuttings, and have moved from chalk soil to acid,
where even the chalk lovers such as Sage, Thyme and Rosemary
have, in the good-natured way of herbs, settled down without
complaint. Perhaps sufficient chalk stayed with them, perhaps they
found building rubble where they grew, perhaps they just did not
mind. I have found that my plants have been most tolerant of my
methods; some have been dug up and replanted in all the wrong
conditions, sown at the wrong times, and heeled cuttings taken
without thought to season. But then herbs do not as a rule care very
much for pampering or the best soils, and in many cases are better
off without either. My Borage fell full length the day I hoped to
draw it, and lay roots exposed long enough for the branches to turn
upwards to the sun. I propped it up, and a week later it was
progressing strongly, and went on, despite its split stem, to flower

for three more months and reach a height of over forty inches.

There are, however, sensible and proper methods for growing herbs. Each plant will have its notes for growing, but there are some generalisations worth knowing. It is tedious but a good thing to sow seeds just below soil level in boxes of soil mixed with sand, and keep them moist and covered with paper until they shoot. Then separate the stronger seedlings and nurture them till they are big enough to withstand the rigours of the weather and predators outside.

The easiest way of propagation is to take cuttings from mature shoots, or to layer. Pull a shoot from the parent plant, preferably from near the base. The shoot should have a "heel," or be sliced cleanly with a sharp blade (see fig. 1, below). Technically these shoots should be short, but I have not found length to be important. My Rosemary began as a cutting almost two feet long. The leaves at the heel end of the cutting should be stripped off, and that area dipped into rooting powder, shaken to remove excess, then potted or planted directly into the soil. Longish cuttings should be inserted at an angle to lie against a bank of earth, so as to be less easily blown (see fig. 2). Sand mixed with soil will mean that water drains well,

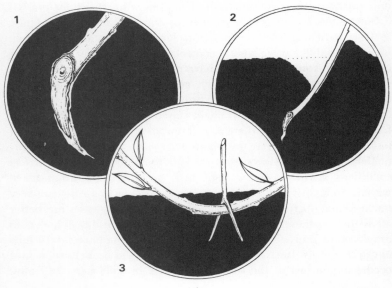

and the young roots can move freely to become established. Layering simply means pinning down a branch so that the central area between main trunk and the bushy tip is covered with soil for about a month, by which time new roots should have grown (fig. 3). Otherwise soil can be built up around small bushy plants so as to cover all but the ends of the branches. If layering is left till late in the year, it is best to leave the new plant attached to its parent until spring, unless it is to be brought indoors, as new roots will have to form when it is replanted, and these will be inhibited by winter. Root division can be a brutal slicing right through a mass of growth, or a more delicate removal of the plant from the earth and a pulling apart of sections.

It is usually quite difficult to realise that a small twig or seedling planted out will really grow to its intended size, so a great effort of will is needed to leave the plant alone in the wilderness around it. But each one will occupy its area quite easily by the end of summer, and will not enjoy being crowded. I have tried to give an approximate area, as well as mentioning those plants which will die down in winter.

Most herbs will grow indoors or in window-boxes, though they will probably be either leggy or stunted, and possibly be more useful for their looks and fragrance than for the quantity of leaf which they can provide in confined space. They need average pots, the bottoms of which are covered with rubble, then filled with a soil mix best obtained from a shop. The pots should stand in containers partly filled with pebbles and some water, so that the plant pots stand on pebbles but out of the water. This provides a moist atmosphere, and the plants should do well if soaked weekly in water till bubbles rise through the soil, and watered occasionally from the top. Indoor plants should be in even temperatures, and draught free.

There is a great deal of research going on as to plant relationships, and the disadvantages and benefits of proximity, which in some cases are considerable. For this book it seems only necessary to say that Dill and Fennel grown close to each other result in much confusion, as they cross-pollinate and the flavours become indistinct. Mints behave similarly, added to which is their likelihood of rust, which would mean the loss of a whole area if one plant became affected. They will also gallop all over the garden if not confined, so need trimming when the runners leave the perimeter of their plot.

Deep vertical digging and pulling of escaped runners will help. Even so, they will probably win, but are definitely worth risking.

Herbs cut for drying should be taken just before flowering, when the oils are at their best, and several inches of the plant should be left to continue growth during summer and autumn when some herbs can be re-cut. Cutting should be done as soon as possible after night moisture has evaporated from the leaves, as they should be quite dry. Hang the lengths upside down in a warm place, or strip the leaves and spread them on racks covered with muslin or paper, where the air can circulate freely, till the leaves are absolutely dry, in about a week. Rub or sieve them, and store in airtight containers out of direct light. When the next year's cuttings are dried, sprinkle what remains of the old dried herbs on to the garden, where they will help new growth.

Pot-pourri makes use of fragrant leaves and flowers which must be dried as just described. Petals should be pulled free from flowers except for rose buds, and only the outer florets of Marigold used. Rose petals and Lavender increase in perfume as they dry. Spices can be added: freshly ground Anise, Caraway, Coriander, and Cloves, also dried peel from oranges and lemons. The lasting fragrant pot-pourri takes considerable time and skill, needing special salts and jars in which the contents can be properly pressed. There are two methods, moist and dry, and for the traditional pot-pourri, colour is not important, as the mixture is kept covered from the light.

Storing herbs for winter depends on the leaves. Most can be deep-frozen, either separately or in mixes such as Bouquet Garni. They may lose colour, and be very brittle when used. Immersing in jars of oil is a good way of preserving herbs, and the oil will become flavoured. For preparing specially flavoured oils, select favourite herbs, crush the leaves and put them into a glass jar; pour in some oil, and a spoonful of wine vinegar, and leave the jar on a sunny shelf for at least two weeks, shaking daily. Herb vinegars probably originated as an attempt to store for winter, and of course resulted in delicious vinegars, which were used in drinks and salads. Flavoured vinegar is made by selecting and preparing herbs as above, but putting them into an opaque container. Only a good wine or cider vinegar will help bring out the flavour; fill the container with some, either heated or cold, and leave out of daylight for at least ten days, shaking occasionally. If either oil or vinegar flavours are weak at the end of this time, more bruised herbs can be added, after straining out the first batch. Seeds from the Umbellifers are, to me, far superior to dried leaves from other herbs in winter, and can be used whole or crushed. Whole they will provide surprises of flavour throughout the dish, crushed and slightly roasted they increase in aroma and will impart a diffused taste. Chervil, Chickweed, Dandelion, Hyssop, Rosemary, Sage, Salad Burnet, Thyme and Winter Savory can be picked fresh all year, though Sage will shed some leaves. Mints and Marjorams will grow under cloches, as will Parsley.

For cooking, fresh herbs should be torn or chopped if the leaves are of any size, and need to be used in much larger quantities than dried herbs, in which the flavour becomes more concentrated.

In making teas, a rough measure is one dried teaspoon or two fresh to one cup, though experience will produce variations according to taste. Boiling water should be poured on to the leaves in the usual way, and left for several minutes to draw. Indian or China tea, or Maté, can be mixed with the leaves, and honey used as a sweetener. Spices such as Nutmeg and Cinnamon or Ginger can be delicious additions, as is the peel of oranges, lemons or grapefruit.

Green vegetables cooked only in the water remaining after washing them seem to retain more flavour, whether simmered or steamed. The former method can result in black saucepans if not carefully watched, and the latter takes time, but both are rewarding. Seasoning with spices and herbs, and lemon juice as well as salt and pepper, or serving with a herb and garlic butter, cheese or cream takes them a long way from the pale drowned "Veg" of tradition.

Green plants are behind everything we eat, somewhere in the food chain. They figure in legends from all lands, and have persisted and flourished throughout history, making their own way despite our interference. They have infinite uses, which include clothing, dyes, and cosmetics, and have recently been credited with the ability to sense mood, and to respond to danger. The fascination is endless. This book touches only a tiny fragment of the plant world, and is simply a pattern, with words.

Meg Rutherford

HERBAL MEDICINE

Ann Warren-Davis

M.N.I.M.H., Consultant Medical Herbalist

I am frequently asked, "What do you call a herb?" My answer is that if you mean, "How many plants have medicinal qualities?" then all plants have virtues, every blade of grass, every root, every piece of bark, every flower, seed, fruit and every bud contain elements which our bodies require, and in a form from which our bodies have evolved by assimilating and metabolising over millions of years.

It is impossible to know all the medicinal virtues and vices of every plant that grows. We have therefore to confine ourselves to a relative handful, a few hundred maybe, which have been used and recognised for several thousands of years. But some plants clearly have more virtues than others.

Homo sapiens has probably always been a combination of carnivore and herbivore. Animals certainly recognise their need for different plants; we have only to watch any domestic animal seek specific herbs, roots or barks if he feels the need for them, to know this.

Man's knowledge of plants presumably grew in much the same way. At first it may have been only a craving or instinct, from which followed empirical knowledge giving traditional usage to many plants. This knowledge was handed down by all tribes and civilisations from century to century, from all parts of the world. Some plants were deliberately grown for their virtues by the monks in their monastery herb gardens, thus acquiring their Latin suffix of *officinale*.

During the Middle Ages, and indeed until this century, the main killer diseases were acute fevers, agues and plagues largely due to the insanitary living conditions and unbalanced feeding habits. During winter months diets were high in salted and other meats, cereals and root vegetables, producing a chronic lack of vitamins. Bad harvests produced starvation for the poor, and consequent malnutrition. In addition frequent brawls, battles, sieges and accidents caused many wounds. It is easy to see therefore that the greatest demand was for vulneraries, fever-reducing agents, gastric- and intestinal-correcting agents, anti-plague agents—little was the humble flea suspected in this case.

Today chronic conditions have taken the place of devastating fevers, and for these conditions small quantities of several herbs are usually more effective than wineglass or cupful doses of one infusion. This traditional method, however, definitely holds its own in acute conditions such as influenza and heavy colds.

Today's medical herbalist needs to have the knowledge required in order to diagnose the cause of a condition, and to decide which herbal agent, combination of herbal agents, diet and living conditions will be required by the body at any one time in order to overcome the situation. Thus there are few specifics, but every herbalist has his or her favourite agents. These agents work slowly and gently, removing toxins which have accumulated in the body, supplying trace elements which have been lacking, astringing one organ, relaxing another, combined according to the understanding and knowledge of the herbalist.

Although a great deal of knowledge has been amassed over centuries from all parts of the world I am sure that there is a vast amount still to be learned and still to be discovered. I am disappointed if a day passes without teaching me something new. It is like an ever-evolving detective story. New problems and conditions arise with every patient, and with every consultation.

In order to get maximum results combinations of plant extracts are usually required, and the knowledge of the number of herbal agents, perhaps six, or ten, or only one, and also the varying quantities, from a fraction of a drop to maybe ten drops in one dose is the essence of the art of the medical herbalist.

Herbal Treatment Centre
34 Cambridge Road
London SW11

MEDICINAL USES

Ann Warren-Davis

Angelica

Leaves, roots, seeds, stalks. Main constituents: a volatile oil, contained in the seed at about 1 per cent, the leaves 0.1 per cent, which partly consists of valeric acid, angelic acid, sugar, a bitter principle, a resin angelicin, which is a stimulant to the lungs and skin. The essential oil of the root contains terpenes. Action: carminative, stimulant, diaphoretic, stomachic, febrifuge, aromatic, tonic, expectorant. The fruits are the strongest. Angelica is used in coughs, colds, pleurisy, rheumatism, wind, colic, and diseases of the urinary organs. It basically comprises a bitter tonic, aromatic stomachic and peptic, which when combined become expectorant, diaphoretic and febrifuge. It is useful in anorexia, dyspepsia and in intestinal meteorism. The yellow juice pressed from the stems helps the pain of rheumatism and gout. It should never be used by diabetics, as it increases the blood sugar content. Externally the leaves are used in compresses for pleurisy and bronchitis, where its action is anti-inflammatory.

Anise

Seed. Main constituents: a fragrant syrupy volatile oil, which contains about 90 per cent anithol, its aromatic constituent, also a fixed oil, mucilage, choline and sugar. Action: carminative, pectoral, expectorant, stomachic, sedative, aromatic, galactagogue, antispasmodic. It is of value in hard dry coughs and hiccoughs, bronchitis and spasms of asthma for which it is immediately palliative when used in hot water. It diminishes the griping of purges, and may be used in flatulence and colic.

Bay *Lauris nobilis*
Leaves, fruit, oil. Main constituents: a greenish volatile oil distilled from the leaves, which contains pinene, geraniol, ugenol and cineol. Action: all parts are excitant and narcotic, the leaves emmenagogue and diaphoretic. Large doses are emetic. Bay was formerly used in hysteria, amenorrhoea and flatulent colic, but is today used only for culinary purposes.

Borage
Leaves and flowers. Main constituents: potassium and calcium combined with mineral acids. Stems and leaves contain a saline mucilage. Fresh juice contains approximately 30 per cent of potash. Action: diuretic, demulcent, emollient. Borage is most useful where its saline qualities are required. It activates the kidneys, and is mostly used in catarrhs, fevers and pulmonary complaints. Its demulcent qualities are due to its mucilage. Its leaves may be used for external poultices.

Caraway
Fruit. Main constituents: 4 to 7 per cent volatile oil. Action: fruit and oil have aromatic, stimulant and carminative properties. Caraway is a carminative cordial, principally employed as an adjunct to other medicines. It is a pleasant stomachic. Flatulent indigestion is relieved by a drop of the oil on a lump of sugar, or a drop in a teaspoonful of water. A poultice of the powdered seed may be used for bruises.

Catmint
Flowering tips. Action: carminative, tonic, diaphoretic, refrigerant, slightly emmenagogue, antispasmodic, mildly stimulating. Catmint produces free perspiration, and is therefore useful in colds and fevers. This tea induces sleep without increasing the heat of the system, and is therefore useful in restlessness, colic, insanity and nerv-

ousness, and is a mild nervine, which can be given to children, two to three teaspoonfuls of an infusion made with one ounce to a pint of boiling water being given frequently. Large doses are emetic.

Chamomile

Common C., flowers. Main constituents: volatile oil, anthemic acid, tannic acid, a glucoside and angelic and tiglic acids, amyl and isobutyl alcohols. Action: tonic, stomachic, anodyne, antiseptic, anti-neuralgic, carminative, sedative. Chamomile tea is an excellent bitter and aromatic carminative for many types of dyspepsia, spastic colics, and nervous and hysterical conditions. *Wild or German C.,* flowers. Main constituents: volatile oil, and a bitter extractive, tannic acid. Action: carminative, tonic. Excellent for children as a sedative and tonic of the gastro-intestinal tract. It can be used in convulsions, stomach disorders and fomentation, dentition and earache. A teaspoonful of a weak infusion can be given at intervals, according to the age and size of the baby.

Chickweed

The whole plant. Main constituents: saponins, calcium oxalate. Action: demulcent, refrigerant, anti-rheumatic, emollient, vulnerary. Chickweed is generally used in ointments, or externally as a poultice for carbuncles, skin eruptions and abscesses. The distilled water is useful for cooling wounds and suppurations.

Chives *Allium schoenoprasum*

The whole plant. Main constituents: a pungent volatile oil, which is rich in sulphur like all the onion family, and causes its distinctive smell and taste.

Comfrey

Root and leaves. Main constituents: abundant mucilage, which contains the healing agent allantoin and also tannin and starch. Action: demulcent, cell-proliferant, astringent, expectorant, vulnerary. Comfrey is valuable wherever there is internal haemorrhage, and is useful in pulmonary complaints, in ruptures and ulceration. It makes excellent ointments, and used externally will help heal fractures and ulcers. It can be used in any condition requiring an astringent mucilage, in lung infections, quinsy, whooping cough, diarrhoea and dysentery. It can be taken as a drink made from the crushed root boiled in milk or water, or in the form of an infusion of the leaves. It is best drunk by the wineglassful, at frequent intervals. As a poultice it reduces the pain and swelling of inflammations.

Coriander
Fruit, fresh leaves. Main constituents: its active ingredient is volatile oil. It also contains malic acid, tannin, and a fatty matter. Action: stimulant, aromatic, carminative. It is mainly used as a flavouring medium to disguise the taste of purgative and correct griping. It may be used in windy colics. The seeds are narcotic if used freely.

Cumin
Fruit. Main constituents: volatile oil. The fruit tissue contains a fatty oil with resin, mucilage, gum, malates, and albuminous matter. Action: Cumin is a stimulant, carminative, antispasmodic, which was considered superior to Fennel and Caraway.

Dandelion
Roots, leaves. Main constituents: a crystalline substance, taraxacin, gluten, potash, gum and up to 25 per cent inulin in autumn, a sugar which replaces the starch. Action: Diuretic, tonic and slightly astringent. Taraxacum is excellent in liver disorders, especially congested liver, and gall stones, as it increases the production of bile. The drink made from roasted and ground root can be slightly laxative.

Dill
Dried ripe fruit. Main constituents: essential oil, similar in odour to Caraway, and with an almost identical composition. The oil consists almost entirely of limonene and carvone, but Dill contains less of the latter. Action: stimulant, aromatic, carminative, stomachic. Dill is a common remedy for children. Dill water is used for flatulence in infants or as a vehicle for children's medicines.

Elder
Bark, leaves, flowers, berries. Main constituents: alkaloid sambucine, a purgative resin, a glucocide sambunigrin, sugars, potas-

sium nitrate. Flowers contain a semi-solid volatile oil. Action: diuretic, sudorific. All parts of the Elder may be used. The inner bark is purgative, and in large doses emetic. The leaves are useful in healing ointments. The flowers make an excellent distilled water, useful for mild sunburn, skin eruptions, freckles, eye inflammations and cosmetics. The flowers also make an invaluable infusion, which can be used as a pleasant beverage, but whose main use is in simple fevers and influenza, and in eruptive disorders such as measles and scarlet fever. The berries can be used as a hair dye, and as a syrup, and to make a rob, or thick jam, useful as a hot cordial for winter colds.

Fennel

Leaves, roots. Main constituent: volatile oil. Fennel can be employed to allay the griping of purges. Fennel water has properties similar to Anise and Dill. With bicarbonate of soda and syrup it forms gripe water, employed for infants' indigestion and wind. The volatile oil contains the properties in concentration. Fennel tea is carminative. A syrup may be made with the expressed juice, useful in chronic coughs.

Hyssop

The whole plant. Main constituents: volatile oil, used by perfumers. Action: expectorant, diaphoretic, sedative, carminative. Hyssop has many uses. In bronchitis and the common cold it is useful after the inflammatory period has passed; it is excellent in sub-acute and chronic bronchitis and nasal catarrh. Its action is due to its essential oil, eliminated via the mucosa, which it liquifies.

Lemon Balm

The whole plant. Main constituents: balsamic oils, resins. Action: carminative, diaphoretic, febrifuge, sedative, antispasmodic. Melissa is mainly useful in flatulent dyspepsia, depressive illness and neurasthenia. It makes a beautifully cooling infusion for fevers and catarrh and influenza, when lemon peel and honey may be added. It is excellent in colds, it eases gout, it cleanses sores.

Lovage

Roots, leaves, seeds. Main constituents: a volatile oil, angelic acid and resin, a bitter extractive, and a colouring principle. Action: aromatic, stimulant, diaphoretic. Lovage can be used in disorders of the stomach and feverish attacks. The leaves are an emmenagogue. An infusion can be made of the leaves.

Marigold

Flowers, leaves. Action: stimulant, diaphoretic, detergent. Invaluable in suppurative conditions, chronic ulcers, varicose veins, and any condition that requires cleansing of the blood stream such as measles, chicken-pox, shingles. The expressed juice can be used on warts, and bee and wasp stings.

Marjoram

Origanum vulgare, the whole plant. Main constituents: a volatile oil, separated by distillation (red oil of thyme is frequently sold as oil of Origanum). Action: stimulant, carminative, diaphoretic, mildly tonic, emmenagogue. Infusions of marjoram are useful for relieving nervous headaches. It produces a gentle perspiration, and brings out eruptions, such as measles; it is of value in spasms, colic, and dyspepsia. *Origanum marjorana, O. onites;* these varieties are stronger fragrant balsamics, warm bitter aromatics. They are sudificants and antispasmodic. Small doses produce gastric secretion and intestinal motility, they are peptic carminatives.

Mint

Spearmint, the whole plant. Main constituents: carvone, which is the chief constituent of the oil, also phellandrine, inactive limonene, dihydrocarveol acetate, esters of acetic, butyric, camphoric or caphoylic acids. Action: it is said to whiten teeth and strengthen nerves and sinews. It is stimulant, carminative, and antiseptic like Peppermint, but less powerful. The distilled water relieves hiccoughs, flatulence, and the giddiness of indigestion. It is a pleasant tea in fevers and inflammatory diseases. It allays nausea and the pain of colic. Peppermint, the whole plant. Main constituents: volatile oil which contains menthol, methyl acetate, isovalerianate, menthone, cineol and terpenes. Action: Peppermint has the same uses as Marjoram, but its antiseptic powers are very marked. It relieves pain which arises from the alimentary canal. It is stimulant, stomachic and carminative, and therefore valuable in dyspepsia, flatulence, colic, abdominal cramps, diarrhoea; it prevents the griping of purgatives, and allays nausea and sickness, and raises internal heat, thereby causing perspiration. It is helpful in palpitations, and is a useful infant cordial.

Nettle

The whole plant. Main constituents: ascorbic acid, formic acid, mucilage, mineral salts, ammonia, carbonic acid, phosphates, a trace of iron, indolic compounds, including histamine and 5-hydroxytryptamine. Action: astringent, anti-haemorrhagic, diuretic, stimulating tonic. Nettle has been used in many conditions. It can be useful in nose-bleeding, skin eruptions, diarrhoea, eczema, asthma, and rheumatism among others, and as a cardiotonic. By-products are sugar, starch and protein.

Parsley *Carum petroselinum*

The whole plant. Main constituents of root: starch, mucilage, sugar, volatile oil and apiin. Parsley seeds contain more volatile oil than the root. This oil contains terpenes and apiol to which the activity of the root is due. Action: carminative, tonic, aperient, chiefly diuretic. Two-year shoots are used, from which a strong decoction is made and used for gravel, stone, kidney congestion, dropsy, jaundice and arthritis. The leaves may also be similarly used, but are generally infused.

Pennyroyal

The whole plant. Main constituents: volatile oil, oil of pulegium. Action: carminative, diaphoretic, stimulant, emmenagogue, antiseptic. Pennyroyal is useful for sudden chills and colds, for spasm, hysteria, flatulence and nausea, by virtue of the fact that it warms the stomach.

Rose

Petals, leaves. Main constituents: a volatile oil, gallic acid, a glucocide quercitrin. Action: bland, astringent, antiseptic. The extract, and decoction of deep red *R. Gallica* are used, for making syrups for sore throats, and whenever a gentle astringent antiseptic is required. The distilled water has many uses, for sore eyes, skin lotions, ointments, liniments and skin conditions. Rose-petal vinegar is said to ease headaches caused by hot sun. An extract can also be made from the leaves. *R. Damascena* is mainly grown in Hungary for the perfume industry in the production of Attar of Roses. The climate and soil conditions of one area being exceptionally suitable for high content of this essential oil. *R. Centifolia* is used mainly in France for the distillation of rosewater; medicinally it has slightly aperient properties, while most other roses are slightly astringent.

Rosemary

Stems, leaves, and oil distilled from the flowering tips. Main constituents: tannic acid, resin. A bitter principle, volatile oil, borneol and other esters, a camphor similar to myrtle, cineole, pinene and camphene. Action: tonic astringent, diaphoretic, stimulant. Rosemary is an excellent stomachic and nervine, which has carminative properties due to its volatile oil. It is renowned for anything to do with the head, for hair-washing, hair lotions. It stimulates the brain, kidneys and nervous system, it is therefore good for nervous depression.

Sage

The whole plant. Main constituents: volatile oil, hydrocarbon pinene, cineol and borneol esters, ketone thujone, the active principle of which helps the animal substances to resist putrefaction. Action: stimulant, astringent, tonic, carminative, antiseptic, emmenagogue. Sage is mostly used as a condiment. It can be used in dyspepsia and makes an excellent gargle boiled with malt vinegar and water: one ounce of Sage to half a pint of vinegar, boil gently for ten minutes, and add an equal quantity of water. This can be used for relaxed throat or infected tonsils, or for an ulcerated throat. The infusion can be used for bleeding gums as a mouthwash. Small repeated doses will help in the delirium of fevers, as it is a stimulant tonic in debility. The tea helps in bilious conditions, in liver and kidney disorders, in colds, quinsy, lethargy, joint pains, palsy, and the excessive perspiration of phthisis. It helps clear mucus from the respiratory organs. Sage leaves can be chewed for ague—in a Sussex remedy five leaves were recommended to be chewed on nine consecutive mornings. Sage is useful in ovarian disfunction, as a stimulant in dyspeptic atonia, and as a bland astringent and antiseptic. It is therefore an excellent mouthwash. Sage tea has been known to lower blood sugar in diabetics. Its essential oil is used for many embrocations, especially for rheumatism, and the leaves can be used for poultices and fomentations. A drink for hot summer days may be made with a few sprigs, a tablespoonful of honey, and the juice of a lemon, by pouring boiling water over the sprigs, dissolving the honey in the liquid, and when cool straining and adding the lemon juice.

Salad Burnet
The whole plant. Action: astringent, tonic, vulnerary. It can· be used in treating diarrhoea, dysentery, haemorrhages and leucorrhoea.

Savory
The whole plant. Action: Summer Savory is aromatic, carminative, and can be used for colic and flatulence. The expressed juice is said to help relieve wasp and bee stings. Winter Savory is aromatic and carminative, and can be used for colic.

Sweet Cicely
Whole plant and seeds. Action: aromatic, stomachic, carminative, expectorant. This is a harmless plant, used for coughs and flatulence. It is a gentle stimulant for debilitated stomachs. The fresh root may be used in an infusion with brandy and water. The roots are antiseptic, the distilled water diuretic. It is helpful in pleurisy. The plant makes a useful ointment for green wounds and ulcers and eases the pain of gout.

Tarragon
The whole plant. Main constituents: essential volatile oil, chemically identical to Anise, which is lost in dried herb. Action: cordial, aromatic. It induces appetite; the root in some places is used to calm toothache.

Thyme
The whole plant. Main constituents: essential oil which contains phenols thymol and carvacrol, also cymene and pinene, menthone, borneol and linalol. The value of the oil depends on the quantity of phenols, especially thymol. Action: antispasmodic, tonic, carminative. Thyme has an antiseptic and balsamic action, which arrests

gastric fermentation. It has antibiotic qualities against some staphylococci and bacilluscoli. It is therefore an excellent intestinal antiseptic, useful in wind spasm and colic. It assists in the promotion of perspiration, in catarrhal colds and sore throats, and is of great value in catarrhal bronchitis and whooping cough.

Violet

Leaves and flowers. Main constituents: mucilage, saponins, high ascorbic acid. Action: slightly laxative, expectorant, emollient, anti-neoplastic. The fresh juice from pressed violet leaves has a great reputation for protecting the body from the spread of tumours. Ascorbic acid is exceptionally high. Violet leaves are also a useful expectorant in any catarrhal infection of the respiratory tract.

MEDICAL TERMS

Unless otherwise specified all infusions mentioned are made at the rate of one ounce to one pint of boiling water, and the dose one wineglassful taken three times daily.

Anodyne eases pain.

Antiseptic destroys bacteria.

Antispasmodic relieves cramps and pains.

Aperient is mildly laxative.

Aromatic a fragrant smell, and a flavour preferable to, and used to disguise, that of other medicines.

Astringent causes tissues to contract.

Carminative corrects flatulence; eases griping pains.

Cordial invigorates.

Demulcent soothes the alimentary tract.

Detergent cleanses.

Diaphoretic promotes perspiration.

Diuretic promotes increase of urine.

Emmenagogue encourages menstrual flow.

Emollient used externally for softening and soothing tissue.

Expectorant loosens phlegm etc. in the chest and nasal passages and induces its expulsion.

Febrifuge reduces fever.

Pectoral promotes relief in diseases of the lungs or chest.

Purgatives cause more vigorous evacuation from the bowels than do laxatives.

Refrigerant cools blood, reduces fever.

Stimulant produces vital activity in various parts of the body.

Stomachic invigorates the stomach and stimulates the appetite.

Sudorific induces perspiration.

Tonic invigorates and strengthens the system.

Vulnerary is used for healing of wounds.

A Pattern of Herbs

HERBS FROM
VARIOUS FAMILIES

Borage
Borago officinalis

Boraginaceae

Young Borage forms a group of coarse leaves with hairy stalks, whose widely spaced veins and crinkled look remind me of an elephant's skin. From the centre rises a stout hairy hollow stem, branching alternately. The lower leaves have stalks, the sides of which are thinly winged and stretch for some way down the main stem below the leaf junction. The whole plant is covered with stiff white hairs, and the leaves are papery to touch. The flowers form as a furry group of buds extending slowly outwards into a pair of flowering stems, on each of which the flowers bloom in turn, one discarding its petals as another opens from the progressing group of buds before it. The flowers are an almost luminous blue, star-shaped, with a white inner area from which stands a central cone of dark stamens. Borage will flower for three months or more, from July to October, if planted in April or May. Common names include Beebread and Star-flower. The leaves may be confused with those of Foxglove, which is *poisonous,* but if there is any doubt about the veins (see p. 6) and the leaf margins, then it is the tough papery feel of the Borage leaves which absolutely distinguishes them from the softly fleshy Foxglove. Other plants have similar leaves (e.g. Elecampine), but in the British Isles at least they are not poisonous.

Habitat and Cultivation: Mediterranean, Middle East, but can sometimes be found wild in waste places in the U.S.A. and the British Isles. Annual. Propagate by seed in spring in a sunny place, and at intervals later to ensure supply. Late sowings may survive mild winters and flower early the following year. They grow to approximately two to three-and-a-half feet high and a little less wide, and if allowed will self-seed abundantly.

Kitchen: Use the leaves when young, either whole or torn, chopped or liquidised. They are coolly fragrant and juicy. The flowers have a delicate taste of nectar, and should be added to salads after the dressing, otherwise their blue will turn to pink. They will retain their colour, however, in aspic, and look marvellous with other decorative topping on aspic surfaces of cold meats etc. **Soups:** Use chopped leaves in Gazpacho, and other vegetable soups (see p. 71). **Salads:** Use both leaves and flowers in green or vegetable mixtures, or in mayonnaise, sour cream or yoghurt. **Vegetables:** Leaves can be cooked as spinach, or one or two may be dipped whole into batter and fried as fritters. Borage is one of the old Pot Herbs (see p. 105). **Meat:** Leaves can be rolled and stuffed, then baked, using fillings of savoury rice or mince, and served with an egg and lemon sauce. **Cheese:** Add finely chopped leaves to cream cheese. **Drinks:** Tea, hot or cold, can be made from the leaves, to which flowers can be added while serving. In cool drinks liquidised leaves can be added to fruit juices or lemonade. **Winter:** Use dried or deep-frozen leaves. **Other Uses:** For jellies for use with meat or on bread, add liquidised leaves to chicken stock and gelatine with seasonings, or, gelatine, lemon juice and sweetener.

BORAGE: silhouette of a particularly robust plant.

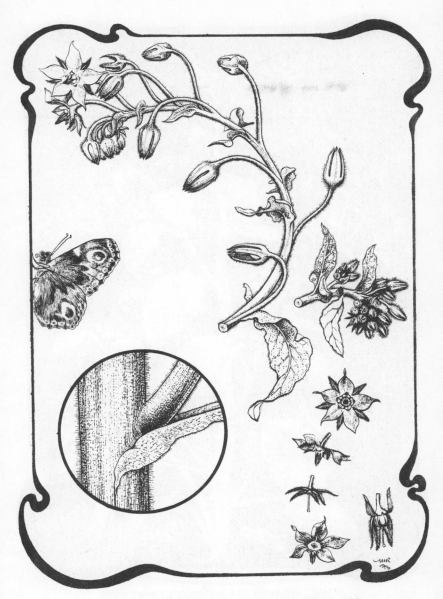

BORAGE: details of flowering stalk, flowers and branching.

5

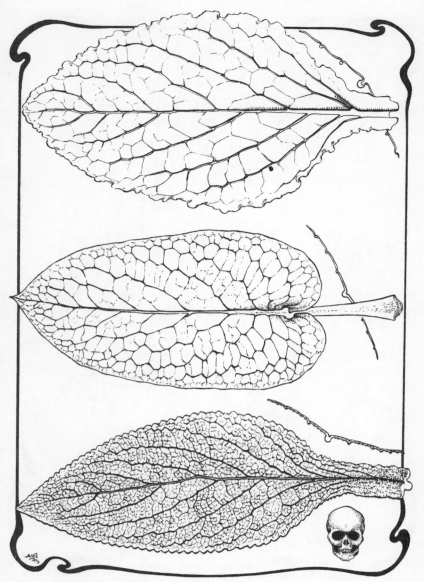

Comparison of young leaves. From top to bottom: Borage, Comfrey and the poisonous Foxglove, with its serrated leaves, and soft silken bloom of hairs.

Comfrey

Symphytum officinale

Boraginaceae

The young Comfrey forms a rosette of handsome stalked and pointed leaves which spring gracefully outwards. One or more central hollow spikes rise from this, carrying leaves gradually less stalked but with a thin wavy leaf margin beside the stalk (as Borage), and extending downstem past the point of attachment. Upper leaves are quite small and stand wing-like on the flowering stems. The whole plant is covered with fine bristly hairs, and the leaves feel papery, as Borage, and are brittle. Comfrey reaches a height of two to four feet. The bell-shaped flowers form on pairs of curling stalks, with one flower alone at the point of the V. The stalks gradually unwind, holding tightly closed buds ahead of open flowers, while seeds form where the flowers have been discarded. The plant is in bloom from May to autumn, and the petals vary in colour from blue-purple, pink to creamy white. Common names include Knitbone and Bruisewort.

Habitat and Cultivation: Europe, temperate Asia, the British Isles, the U.S.A. and Canada. Moist areas beside water, low fields, semi-shade. Perennial, dies down in winter. Propagate by seed or cuttings in spring, root division in autumn. New plants will shoot from any

COMFREY: whole plant, showing changes in shape of leaf and leaf bases, from first to final growth.

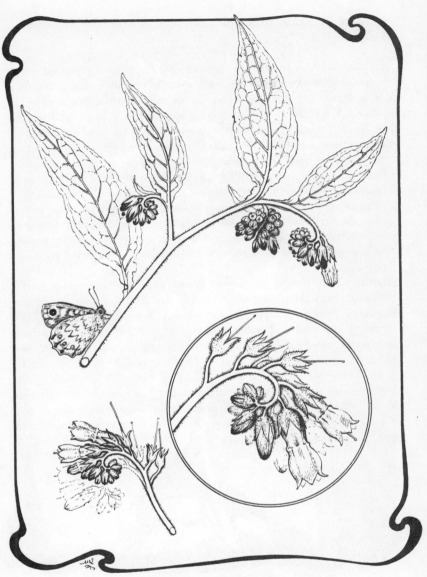

COMFREY: detail, with enlarged flowering stalks.

portion of the brittle root, which can make it very difficult to eradicate.

Kitchen: Use the young leaves, whole for fritters, or chopped, torn or liquidised. The roots are used crumbled and roasted. **Salads:** Young leaves are good in salads or in mayonnaise, sour cream or yoghurt. **Vegetables:** Young shoots and leaves cooked as spinach will be mucilaginous and require no butter but some seasoning. Fritters are made by dipping one leaf, or two together, into batter and frying. Leaves can have fillings (savoury rice, mince etc.) placed on them, then be rolled and baked, and served with egg and lemon sauce, or cheese sauce. **Drinks:** The root, crumbled and roasted in the oven till brown (1½ to 4 hours, depending on the oven, which should be slow) can be ground and mixed with Dandelion root, similarly treated. They combine to make a pleasant brown drink, sometimes called substitute coffee. **Winter:** Use dried roots.

Another Fish Broth: Set some Water over the Fire in a kettle proportioned to the Quantity of Broth you would make; put in the Roots of Parsley, Parsnips, and whole Onions, all Sorts of Pot Herbs, a Handful of Parsley, and Sorrel and Butter; let the whole be well seasoned; then put in the Bones and Carcases of Fish, the Flesh of which you have used for Farces, and also the Tripes of them, being well clean'd, some Tails of Crawfish pounded in a Mortar, and four or five Spoonfuls of the Juice of Onions; let this be all well seasoned and boiled, then strain it through a Sieve; put it back into the Kettle, and keep it hot to simmer your Soops, to boil your Fish and other Things.

Chickweed
Stellaria media

Caryophyllaceae

A low sprawling plant, with soft pale stems only able in some conditions to lift themselves more than a few inches from the ground. The leaves are in pairs, the lower smaller and stalked, those towards the flowers being grouped closer together and stalkless. Flowers are tiny, with five petals so deeply cut as to make them look ten, and shorter than the sepals. The latter are hairy and so thin at the edges that they become transparent. The flower stalk is very short while the flower is blooming, but as the seed develops the stalk extends and droops into the wind. There are several similar plants of the same family, and Chickweed can vary tremendously according to soil and situation. But apart from its tiny flowers, *Stellaria media* is distinguished by a single very fine and immaculately straight line of hairs which runs the length of the stem, changing sides at each leaf junction. It flowers all year round and is sometimes known as Starweed.

Habitat and Cultivation: Found throughout the temperate regions of the world, where it has been carried by various civilisations. Found in profusion in waste places, hedgerows and cultivated and open ground. Annual, evergreen. Propagation: can be transplanted but is readily available in most gardens or waysides. Usually about three inches high and one foot wide, but it can vary enormously.

Kitchen: Use the whole plant, leaves and stems. The latter look stringy when cooked, so I prefer them liquidised or chopped. The flavour is very mild, so improves with seasoning or herb butters. **Salads:** Whole young plants thoroughly washed, can be eaten raw and mixed with other salads. Leaves can be stripped from the stem first. **Vegetables:** Cooking reduces the bulk of Chickweed by about two-thirds, so a few large handfuls are required for each person. Cook for about 4 minutes, tossing frequently. Serve with herb butters to lift the flavour, and with Chives, garlic, Mint, onion, or seeds such as Coriander, Cumin, Fennel, as well as pepper and salt. **Winter:** The whole plant is available fresh.

To Make Pottage the French Way: Take hard Lettuce, Sorrel and Chervil, of each a like Quantity, or any other Herbs you like, as much as a half Peck will hold press'd down, pick, wash them and drain them, put them into a Pot with a Pound of fresh Butter, and set them over the Fire, and as the Butter melts, stir them down in it, 'till they are all as low as the Butter; then put in some Water, a little Salt, some whole Cloves, and a Crust of Bread, and when it is boil'd, take out the Crust of Bread, and put in the Yolks of a Couple of Eggs well beaten, and stir them together over the Fire; lay into a deep Dish some thin Slices of white Bread, pour it in, serve it up.

CHICKWEED: using chicken for scale, shows variable stem sizes and enlarged flower.

Elder

Sambucus nigra

Caprifoliacae

A shrub, with soft woody trunk, pithy interior and cork-like bark, carrying pinnate leaves opposite each other on a stalk with a single leaf at the top. Flowers have mostly five petals, but frequently only three or four, and form in frothy gatherings of tiny perfumed heads on stems of varied length which rise from a central stalk, forming an almost level platform. Fruit follows, becoming a black shiny berry. When the flowers bloom in June and July the normally strong-smelling bush is surrounded by their sweet fragrance.

Habitat and Cultivation: Europe, W. Asia, British Isles. Similar and apparently related shrubs are found wild in the U.S.A. and appear to have similar properties. In hedgerows, woods and sunny waste places. Perennial, deciduous. Propagate by cuttings in autumn or spring. Size usually corresponds with that of the hedge about it, or up to about thirty feet.

Kitchen: Use flowers and berries. **Salads:** Open or unopened flower heads, removed from the stem can be mixed with green or fruit salads. **Drinks:** Tea can be made from the flowers, wine from flowers or berries. A cool drink can be made by filling a container with flowers, adding boiling water, and allowing it to cool. **Winter:**

dried flowers can be used for drinks. **Other uses:** Flower heads can be made into fritters. Hold by the stalk and dip into batter, then lift into a pan to fry, cutting off the stem when it has settled. The result is delicate and sweet. Berries can be used in puddings, jams and jellies. They combine well with other fruit, especially gooseberries in jams and pies.

To Carbonado, Broil or Roast Beef, the Italian Way: Having got Ribs of Beef, cut them into Steaks, and back them; then sprinkle them with Rose-Vinegar, and Elder Vinegar, and season them with Salt, Pepper, and Coriander-seed, then lay them one upon another in a Dish for an Hour, and broil them on a Gridiron, or toast them before the Fire, and serve them up with the Gravy that came from them, or the Gravy and Juice of Orange boiled together.

To Stew Cockles: Having got some Cockles, stew them with Claret, Capers, Rose, or Elder Vinegar, Wine Vinegar, large Mace, gross Pepper, grated Bread, minced Thyme, the Yolks of hard Eggs minc'd, and Butter; stew them well together. Thus you may stew Scollops, but leave out Capers.

To Dress Fresh Herrings: Gut them through the Gills, wash them, rub them over with melted Butter, drudge them with Crumbs of Bread, and broil them on a Gridiron: Make your Sauce of Vinegar, Butter, Salt, Pepper, and Mustard. Or else you may brown some Butter, and shred some sweet Herbs very small, and put into it; season with Vinegar, Salt, Pepper, Anchovies, and Capers.

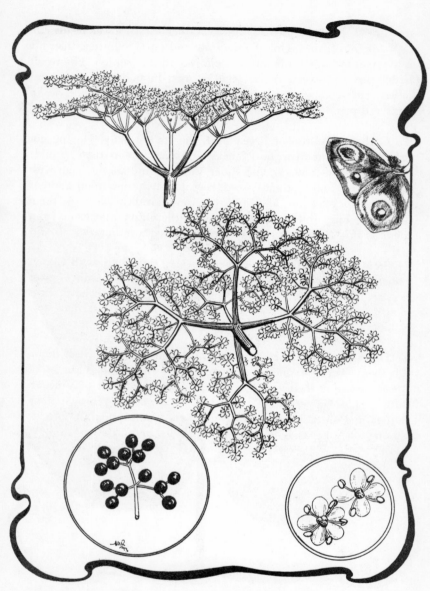

ELDER: flowering head; enlarged flowers showing variation in numbers of petals and berries.

ELDER: leaf stems usually have two or three pairs of leaves plus the terminal leaf.

Stinging Nettle   *Urticaceae*

(Greater) *Urtica dioica*
(Lesser) *Urtica urens*

Surely the Stinging Nettle is familiar to everyone, but what may not be so well known is that it has a host of imitators, none of which are related, and which do not sting. These like to live in the proximity of Nettles and so protect themselves from plunder. While the Nettle and its followers all have opposite pairs of leaves, the distinctions are very simple. The Nettle has a rounded, somewhat grooved stem, and the notable feature here is that the leaves attach to the *rounded* section, while the Deadnettles have square stems and the leaves attach to the *flats*. The latter belong to the Mint family, the *Labiatae*, and thus have lipped flowers, ranging in colour from purple to white or yellow, placed in whorls about the stem above the leaf junctions, and are pollinated by insects. Nettles have trailing tassels of tiny pale green flowers which are pollinated by the wind. The White Deadnettle without its flowers can look particularly like Nettles, and it may take some courage to touch the broad serrated leaves, despite the square stem. But when carrying its elegant white flowers it is utterly distinctive at a glance. Deadnettles flower from early spring onwards, Nettles from June onwards.

Habitat and Cultivation: Temperate regions of the world, in waste places and hedgerows, usually in good soil. Greater is perennial, with a creeping rootstock. Lesser is annual; both die down in winter. Propagation would no doubt be by root division, but with such an abundance of Nettles in the wild, this should hardly be necessary. Elimination is usually the concern of most people.

Kitchen: Leaves and young stems, picked with rubber gloves and scissors, washed and finely chopped or liquidised. The plant loses all trace of the stinging hairs once cooked, and provides one of the most nutritional meals. It is important to use young growth in spring only, preferably almost the whole plant when only about four to six inches high. Later in the season the leaf structure becomes granular and unpleasant. Nettles diminish their volume by about two-thirds during cooking. **Soups:** A really delicious soup is made by melting butter in a saucepan, adding flour for thickening, which should bubble for a few moments while being stirred, before boiling chicken stock is added and the whole mixed thoroughly till smooth, and of the right consistency. Add liquidised Nettles, seasoning, and cook for up to ten minutes, then add soured cream, and chopped herbs if desired. Makes a deep green and inviting soup. **Vegetables:** Simmer leaves in a very little water and butter for fifteen to twenty minutes, strain if juice remains (and save the juice for soups etc.), serve with ordinary or herb butter, or spices and salt and pepper. **Drinks:** Infusions can be made from the leaves.

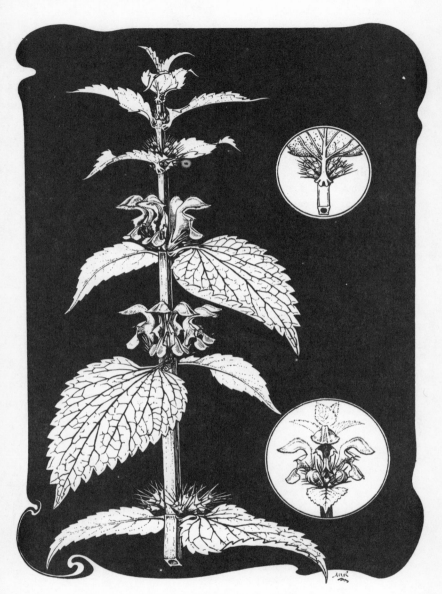

WHITE DEADNETTLE (hairs omitted).

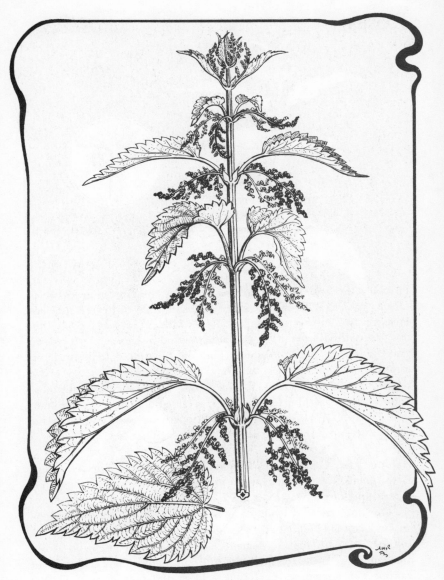

STINGING NETTLE (hairs omitted).

Roses   *Rosaceae*

Probably the best Rose of all for eating is the Apothecaries' Rose (*Rosa gallica,* Provens Rose), with stunning deep red flowers. Perhaps the most beautiful is Rosa Mundi (*Rosa gallica versicolor*), with its petals so casually marked with strips of red on pink, fading to pink on white. The one illustrated opposite is an unusually large specimen, as they generally only grow to about three-quarters that size. Cabbage Roses (*centifolia*) and Damask (*damascena*) are also excellent for petals and hips, as is the common Dogrose (*Rose canina*) found in our hedgerows and flowering from June, hips forming in late August or September.

Habitat and Cultivation: Originally a native of the Northern Hemisphere, Roses now grow in all temperate regions of the globe, an example of the way man has taken plants with him on his travels. Our domesticated Roses stem from the East, in and around Persia, and China, then Japan, changing gradually as the plants were cultivated in different settlements along the way. The wild Roses are found in hedgerows, fields, and on banks. The Dogrose of Europe can sometimes be found wild in the northeastern United States and nearby Canada. Perennial. Propagation varies; it is perhaps best to acquire Roses from nurseries, and plant them in

ROSA MUNDI (*Rosa gallica*).

23

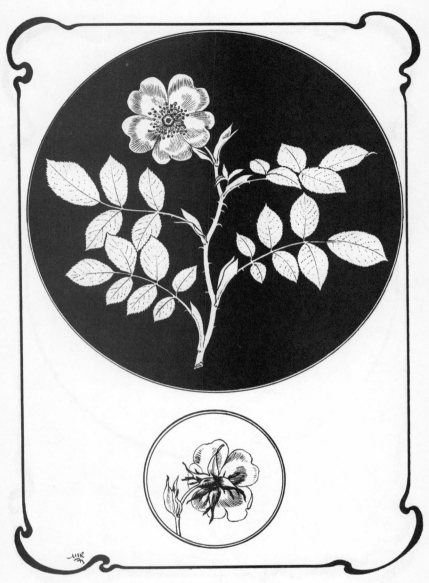

DOGROSE (*Rosa canina*).

LA REINE VICTORIA (Bourbon).

25

well-drained soil in a sunny spot, pruning well back at first. Size will depend largely upon situation; usually they vary from four to ten feet high.

Kitchen: Any Rose with a good perfume can be used for cooking, but usually it is the older types which are preferred. Those with deep red petals are generally more fragrant, so will be more satisfactory. The qualities of the petals increase in strength as they dry, making them particularly valuable for pot-pourri. Rose-hips are the fruit of the shrub Roses, Dogrose and Sweet Briar. Petals are used simply as they are, pulled from the flower, and the flavourless base is thrown away. Hips need cooking, and this can entail the long and awful experience of trying to remove the tiny hairs which make up the centre of the fruit. To make syrup, mince, or somehow pulverise the hips, add water and boil. Strain off the cooled liquid through a very fine cloth, return to the stove and re-cook the mixture at least once, and strain again. The resulting juice should be absolutely free of hairs. Simmer to reduce it, adding sugar in the last cooking period to make the juice into a syrup. (A rough proportion of sugar for syrup is just under a pound of sugar to a pint of liquid.) This can be diluted as a drink, blended with other juices; or made with much less sugar, thickened, and used as a cold soup, with petals added before serving. **Salads:** Petals can be mixed with fruit and vegetable salads. **Drinks:** Make syrup as above, or boil whole hips gently in water till they are soft, strain and drink as tea; delicious and highly nutritious. **Winter:** Use dried hips. **Other uses:** Jam is made from the hips, cooked as above except that the quantities are about three cups of sugar to one of hips, and slightly less than one cup of water. Petal jam is really petal jelly: mix fresh petals in a blender with sugar and water in the above proportions till thoroughly smooth, add mixed gelatine and let cool.

Salad Burnet

Poterium sanguisorba

Rosaceae

A fern-like plant, low and bushy when mature, forming a clump of arching pinnate leaves on a sometimes purplish stalk. The flowering stems rise to double the height of the plant, or more, finally collapsing sideways. They are slightly hairy at the base, but smooth and reddish towards the top where the flowers form, first into rounded heads of purplish balls, then opening into tight groups of green petal-less flowers. The upper are female, showing only the fluffy-headed purplish styles. The middle can be both sexes, but the lower are male, and shower long stemmed stamens from their centres. There are similar Burnets, but the Salad B. is easily distinguished when in flower. The Greater Burnet has elongated heads of a deep reddish purple and with no hanging stamens, and each leaf is about two inches long by about one inch wide. Greater B. is found in damp meadows and is in flower from June to September. Salad Burnet has small leaves scarcely more than half an inch long and likes dry pastures, flowering from late spring to August.

Habitat and Cultivation: Europe, British Isles, and introduced to the U.S.A. by settlers. Dry fields, banks and waste areas, chalklands. Perennial, evergreen. Propagate by seed, or division of roots in spring or autumn. A plant about one foot high will double dimensions when the flowering stalks extend. Removal of the heads will control the shape a little and leaves will bush out again leaving more plant to be picked.

Kitchen: Use the leaves, either whole, stripped from the stem, or cut across the stem and leaf, into fragments. They make very good decoration for aspic on cold meats, and the delicate flavour can be complementary. **Soups:** Use in chicken or bland soups, or as a garnish. **Salads:** Add to green, vegetable or fruit salads. **Cheese:** Mix with cream or cottage cheese. **Drinks:** Make tea with the leaves, or use as a decoration in cool drinks. **Winter:** The plant remains in leaf all year round.

Glazed Turbuts: Take a small Turbut, the Bigness of your Dish, gut and wash it, cut off the Fins, and lard it with fine Bacon; take a Stew-pan, put in a Bottle of White Wine, with an Onion sliced, Salt, and sweet-Basil, and put your Stew-pan over a Stove; when your Wine begins to boil, put in your Turbut, and when it has boiled some Time, take it out, and get a Jelly in Readiness made thus: Take some Slices of Veal and Ham, cut in small Pieces, and put them in a Stew-pan, with an Onion cut in Pieces; moisten it with Broth, and put it to boil; being done, strain off your Jelly, put it in a clean Stew-pan over the Fire, and let it boil till it is turned to Caramel, that is, glazed; then put in your Turbut, and put your Pan over hot Cinders, that it may glaze well; being glazed and ready to serve up, put an Italian Sauce in your Dish, with your Turbut over it, and serve it for the first Course.

To Roast a Leg of Mutton with Cockles: Stuff it all over with Cockles, and roast it. Garnish with Horse-radish.

SALAD BURNET: reduced scale (see butterfly); flower much enlarged, leaf
and leaflet natural size when drawn (see bumble-bee).

Sweet Violet   *Violaceae*
Viola odorata

There is a bewildering variety of Violets, but the Sweet V. can be distinguished by the fact that the sepals are almost oblong and rounded at the end, not tapering or sharply pointed, and that the flowering stems are not branched, but spring direct from the root, as do the leaves, and also that the plant is part of a long system of runners, from which fountains of Violets erupt at intervals. (Illustration shows a young plant beginning its progression.) Other Violets may have blunted sepals, but will have branched stems and no runners; only the Sweet Violet has blunted sepals, branchless stalks, and runners. It flowers from February to April, after which its leaves increase to sometimes as much as five times their original area.

The Violet seems quite prepared to sacrifice its flowers as it provides a different kind of flower in autumn, inconspicuous but full of seeds, which are eventually expelled. Nonetheless, the plants should not be plundered; commercial Violets are very good to eat, and wild Violets are increasingly rare.

Habitat and Cultivation: Europe, northern Asia, British Isles and parts of the northeastern United States and nearby Canada. In shady lanes and woodsides, hedgerows. Perennial, evergreen.

Propagate by separating healthy rooted runners from mature plants. Space well apart, leaving about one foot between plants. Ideally, the new plants should go into a position of partial shade in summer, sun and shelter in winter. Plants should be split and renewed each year, otherwise they become overcrowded and may not flower.

Kitchen: Violet leaves and flowers have such a high content of Vitamin C, and the leaves also have Vitamin A, that they are worth experimenting with in the kitchen, but there are two points to note: the plants are slightly laxative, and the flowers change colour if combined with acids and alkalis: lemon juice will turn the juice red, and cream, milk, etc. will remove this rich colour and leave a diminished pale green. The flowers and leaves enhance any salads, and the flowers retain their colour in aspic. They give this colour to water, and if liquidised have many uses. Jelly can be made in the same way as rose-petal jelly (see p. 26), perhaps adding some lemon juice if a redder tone is required. Syrup is made by pouring boiling water on to flowers, letting them stand for a day, then boiling the strained liquid together with lemon juice and sugar. This syrup can be diluted in other fruit drinks, or used as it is. Leaves can be used as a vegetable, either with other greens or with onions and seasonings. The colour change in the flowers unfortunately rules out their visual delight in ice cream but the flavour is delicate and well worth trying.

To Boil a Turbot: Put the Turbot into a Kettle, with White Wine Vinegar, Verjuice, and Lemon, season with Salt, Pepper, Cloves, Onions, and Bayleaf, add to these a little Water, and some Milk, to cause it to boil white; boil it over a gentle Fire: Garnish with Slices of Lemon on the Top, Parsley and Violets, when in season. (Verjuice is the acid juice of sour fruit, crab apples, grapes, etc.)

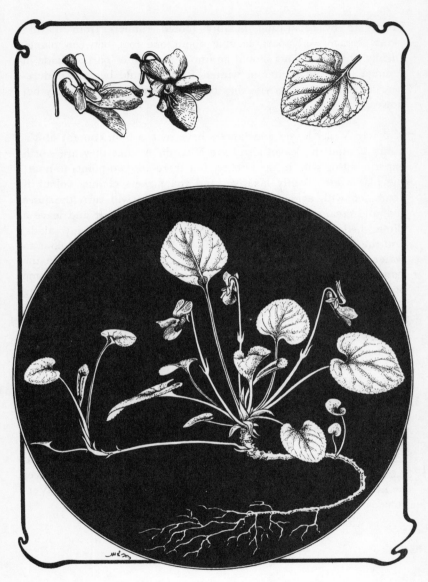

VIOLET: enlarged flowers and whole plant.

32

DAISY FAMILY

DANDELION: showing a plant and silhouette of a typical leaf.

Dandelion
Taraxacum officinale

Compositae

The Dandelion does not entirely blanket the land, there are small areas where it does not grow. Nor are all those golden daisies Dandelions. So many unrelated plants carry similar flowers on similar plants that it can be quite confusing. There are some main points, however, which will distinguish the Dandelion from the others. The hollow flower stem will always be unbranched, and though hairless may be downy, and will taper towards the flower head and the downturned bracts. The leaves also will be hairless, or almost so, and thin and shiny, though the indentations will vary from deeply toothed to almost entire margins. The whole plant is fascinating, with its whorls of leaves so divided as to receive maximum light, and channelled to send water to the roots. The flower is visited by a large variety of insects, but those hoping to plunder from below and perhaps destroy the flower instead of helping with pollination are deterred by the barricade of bracts. The head is very sensitive to light and weather and will close unless the conditions are quite right. The leaves lie flat in low grass or gravel but stand erect in long grass or against obstacles. The very pretty composite flowers show for most of the year, but their full elegance is in spring.

Habitat and Cultivation: All Europe, central Asia, the U.S.A., in almost all grassy areas, pastures, meadows and waste land. Evergreen, though may be infrequent in winter. Propagate by seed, or allow plants to self-sow. (One might say that we have no choice.) Plants can easily be transplanted. It is possible to blanch leaves while the plant is growing, by covering with a pot or planting in a trench and covering with soil when they are established, but green leaves are more nutritious than pale.

Kitchen: Leaves, torn or whole, fresh as a vegetable or dried for drinks, should be picked young, as age makes them bitter. Flowers are used for wine. **Salads:** Torn leaves are used alone or mixed with other salads. **Vegetables:** Leaves can be cooked as spinach, and served similarly, either plain or with butter and other herbs, or with sliced onions, garlic, spices and lemon juice. Young roots can be peeled and boiled, or fried in oil, to make a delicious vegetable. **Drinks:** Make tea from the leaves, wine from the flowers. From the root a very pleasant brown drink is made, for some reason known as coffee substitute. Roots either fresh or dry are broken into smallish pieces and put on a baking tray in the middle of a moderately slow oven. Dried roots will cook quickly, and may take only an hour, but fresh will take longer. The broken pieces need turning at intervals to ensure an even colour, which is a pretty rusty brown, and the air will be permeated with a delicious aroma similar to chocolate sponge. When roasted the roots can be ground and used in any of the ways of making coffee, allowing barely a teaspoon to each cup. I cannot think of it as coffee, but some mix coffee into the dandelion root because they prefer the taste that way. One can use spices such as cinnamon to enhance the flavour, but it can be very pleasant alone. **Winter:** Plants will last through the season. Roots, leaves and flowers can be dried.

Chamomile   *Compositae*

Chamaemelum nobile, or *Anthemis nobilis* (Common Chamomile)
Matricaria recutita (Wild Chamomile, German Chamomile)

Two Chamomiles are used for teas; true or Common C., which has
the single flower shown overleaf, and can be found growing wild.
This is a bitter herb, used medicinally—a less bitter double variety
has been developed under cultivation. The second plant is Wild or
German C., whose pleasant soothing tea is so useful and relaxing. It
is sleep-inducing if taken for several nights.

In the British Isles four Chamomiles grow wild, in the United
States, five. One of these has yellow petals so I have not mentioned
it. The confusion lies amongst the remainder, which have yellow
centres and white petals. They are very similar to the three wild
Mayweeds, though the latter are quite hairless. To add to the confusion the plants are likely to be found growing side by side, and
varying in size and shape with each situation. Common C. is rare. It
is the plant used for lawns where it will release its aroma when
crushed, and will not be allowed to flower. It begins with a bushy
growth from which flowering stalks extend, then the plant becomes
straggly, its buds nodding before they lift into flower, and the foliage is less lush. The stems and leaves are sparsely hairy or downy.
White petals surround the increasingly conical yellow centre and
gradually fall in angle as the centre becomes domed. Its leaves are
similar to those of Yarrow, which form a low green froth before the
main stem rises.

CHAMOMILE: Common C., showing the whole plant with some stems cut away, progression of leaves, and inset flower heads. Opposite, (1) the same plant, head halved, and disc floret with transparent scale, much enlarged; (2) the scale of Stinking C. (*Anthemis cotula*), enlarged; (3) scale of Corn C. (*Anthemis arvensis*), much enlarged; (4) Pineapple Weed, or Rayless C. (*Matricaria matricioides*), with flower and enlarged

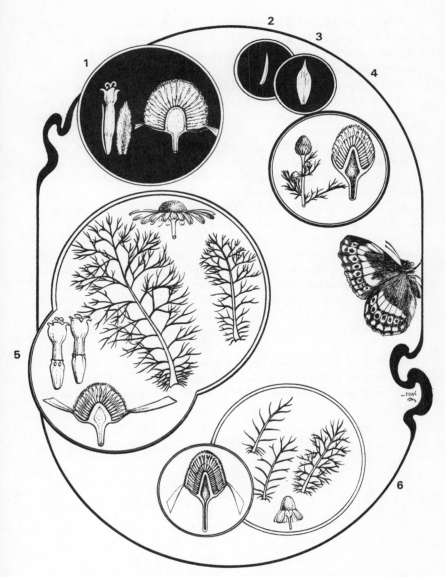

halved head showing hollow receptacle; (5) Scentless Mayweed (*Matricaria inodora*), which is sometimes slightly scented: showing flower, leaves, enlarged halved flower head and two sides of a ray-floret with its two small spots; (6) Wild or German C. (*Matricaria recutita*), with small domed flower head and leaves, and enlarged flower head with hollow receptacle.

Wild C. is altogether a finer plant (see illustrations), despite the variation in size. It is quite hairless, and the flower centres are domed almost from the beginning, making it easy to find the hollow centre when opened.

Attempting to distinguish the Chamomiles has been very difficult, and has resulted in this lengthy description, which seems a lot just for a cup of tea, but it is important that it be the right cup of tea. From my observation Common C. differs from the others in one respect at first glance; the feathery leaflets fold back over the main-stem of the leaf almost as they leave it, whereas all others are more sparsely feathery. This is probably not an infallible guide, as the leaves can become more finely cut by late summer, but it is some help. Wild C. is quite simple; it is the only flower of the group to have both petals and a hollow interior.

Botanists rely on identifying each plant of the seven by the presence or absence of minute and almost transparent scales amongst the ray-florets of the flower, and the shapes of these scales. As they cling to the florets in fresh flowers, and as they are the same colour, and need a very strong lens to be seen at all, this makes as good a case as any for simply buying dried flowers. But I have drawn the scales on page 39 as some guide for explorers.

Habitat and Cultivation: Waste ground, sandy and arable soil. They can be propagated by seed or transplanted, and flower from June to August or beyond. Wild C. is annual, Common C. is perennial.

Marigold, Pot

Compositae

Calendula officinalis

Pot Marigold, with its single, bright orange flowers, and not its showy relations, is the plant used medicinally. A stem sharply angled, usually with four or five sides, supports pale leaves which are without very visible veins, shiny, but not smooth to the touch. Leaves are stalkless, the tapering sides being longer than the midrib as they appear slightly to wrap the mainstem where they join. Seeds appear as a wondrous wormy cluster. Marigolds have a reputation for year-long flowering, but they usually only manage from about April to late autumn.

Habitat and Cultivation: Southern Europe, Asia. Not wild in the British Isles or U.S.A. Annual; propagate by seeds in a sunny spot in spring. They will grow approximately twelve to eighteen inches high and not quite as wide. Continual picking of the flowers will ensure the longest flowering period.

Kitchen: Petals only are used, both for colouring and flavor. **Soups:** Use the pounded petals from three or more flowers to give colour and a subtle flavour to soups, then garnish with more petals. **Salads:** Scatter petals into all types. **Meat:** Use in casseroles and stuffings, particularly with beef, chicken, fish and game. **Cheese:** Mix into

MARIGOLD: the whole plant.

MARIGOLD: flowering top, flower and lower leaf.

cream and cottage cheeses. **Drinks:** Tea made from the petals is not only beautiful but a tonic. **Winter:** Use dried petals. **Other uses:** Petals added to boiling water will colour rice grains, as do Saffron and Turmeric, and leave a pleasant flavor. Petals can also be included in bread and cake mixtures.

Breast of Veal in Galantine: Bone a Breast of Veal, stretch it, and beat it as flat as you can; season it with Parsley, Thyme, Marjoram, Winter-savoury, Marygolds, all well minc'd, Pepper, Salt and Nutmeg; roll it up well, and tie it very close; then tie it up in a Cloth, and boil it in good season'd Broth, Wine, and a little Thyme. When it is boil'd, let it cool in the same Liquor; send it up either Whole or in Slices, upon a Napkin. Garnish it as you like.

To Boil a Leg of Veal: Stuff it with Beef-sewet, and sweet Herbs chopp'd, season'd with Salt and Nutmeg, and boil it in Water and Salt; then take some of the Veal, and put to it some Capers, Currants, whole Mace, a Piece of interlarded Bacon, two or three whole Cloves, some Artichoak Suckers boil'd; and put in beaten Butter, boil'd Marrow, and Mace, and Pieces of Pears. Then take Sorrel, Sage, sweet Marjoram, Thyme and Parsley; mince them coarsly, and bruize them with the Back of a Ladle; put these into your Broth to make it green, and give them a Walm or two, then your other Materials, some Barberries, or Gooseberries, beaten Butter, and Lemon. (Walm is a period of boiling.)

Plumb-Pottage for Christmas: Take two Gallons of strong Broth, put to it two Pounds of Currans, two Pounds of Raisins of the Sun, half an Ounce of sweet Spice, a Pound of Sugar, a Quart of Claret, a Pint of Sack, the Juice of three Oranges and three Lemons; thicken it with grated Biscuits, or Rice Flour, with a Pound of Prunes.

Tarragon   *Compositae*
Artemisia dracunculus (French)
Artemisia dracunuloides (Russian)

Tarragon can grow to three or more feet high, and as a mature plant will be almost as broad. It is both bushy and delicate, with long stems from which pale slender alternate leaves extend, then slightly droop. The two varieties are very similar to look at; the Russian will sometimes bear pronged leaves. The taste is the easy method of distinguishing between them, supposing there is a choice of plants, though the flavour of both plants will change according to circumstance. A cutting from a good Russian bush may thrive but have no flavour one year, and then acquire a good taste next year, and a French Tarragon may diminish gradually with maturity till almost flavourless. Russian has a mild taste, but French has a clear tang which to me seems both spicy and oily, and can almost feel like burning, which is the reason why this herb should be used at first with caution. It is distinguished from Hyssop and Savory by its alternate leaves on round stems; the others have opposite leaves on square stems. Neither Tarragon successfully flowers in the British Isles or France, and if flowers do appear in July or August, they may not open. It is sometimes called Little Dragon.

Habitat and Cultivation: French Tarragon comes from southern Europe, and likes a dry warm position in poor soil. Russian comes from Siberia. Perennial, dies down in winter. Propagate by root division in spring, or cuttings taken during the growing season, into a sunny sheltered position, where roots can be protected in winter. Too much moisture will kill Tarragon. Approximate size for mature French Tarragon will be three feet by three feet, Russian will be somewhat larger.

Kitchen: One of the most desirable herbs, requiring care with quantities at first. Use the leaves or young shoots, chopped, torn or whole. **Soups:** Add finely chopped leaves. **Salads:** Use in all vegetable salads, with avocados or in mayonnaise, sour cream or yoghurt. **Vegetables:** Use with artichokes, asparagus, beans, carrots, courgettes, celeriac, mushrooms, potatoes, salsify, tomatoes. **Meat:** Use with beef, chicken, duck, fish, hare, liver, pork, rabbit, veal and sauces for same, especially Sauce Béarnaise. Also use in herb butters, marinades, pâtés and terrines. **Winter:** Use leaves deep-frozen, dried or stored in vinegar or oil. **Other uses:** Add leaves to omelettes and soufflés. Cook with rice or lentils.

To Dress Soals the Spanish Way: Fry your Soals, and afterwards cut them into Fillets; make a Sauce for them of White Wine, Salt, Pepper, a Couple of Cloves of Garlick, Thyme, and a Bay-leaf. Then soak them by Degrees in the Sauce, and garnish them with what you please.

TARRAGON: flowering tip in bud, branching top, and a branch from mid-way down the plant; also enlarged flowers. The leaf drawings show how the splits may occur, and the way veins form a slightly raised and rounded edge. The veins are not apparent from below, where the appearance is smooth and waxy.

TWO-LIPPED FLOWERS

Basil

Ocymum basilicum

Labiatae

Lovely stories of scorpions are connected with this plant; they were supposed to breed in it, or from it.

Basil (also called Sweet Basil) has an upright square stem, with opposite branches and opposite leaves. The leaves are shiny and frequently bulge between the veins, as if the wind were stretching them. Leaves butt the stem in a small rounded joint with a noticeable junction at its tip, from which the leaf will part very easily. Flowering spikes appear like elegant pagodas, the top of each calyx having a broad flattish cap on its upper side. The buds appear in threes above the leaves, and eventually small white flowers open, showing four rounded shapes on the upper lip, and a long tongue for the lower lip. Basil blooms in August–September. There is a purple variety. Like all *Labiatae*, it attracts bees.

Habitat and Cultivation: Originally from the tropics, Asia, India, Africa and the Pacific but sometimes found growing wild even in the northeast United States and nearby Canada. Annual. Propagation by seeds in spring. Basil can be very difficult to grow and really needs a good summer. Frost will destroy it in spring or autumn, so seedlings should remain protected till as late as June, then put into a sunny place in good, well-drained soil, spaced about one foot

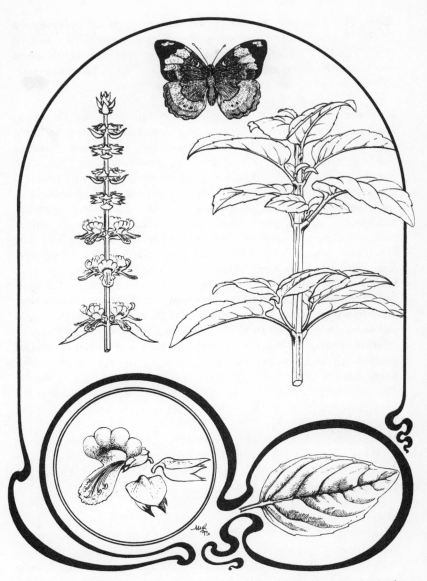

BASIL: flowering spike, leaf stalk, with lines about the leaf base, and a leaf, also the flower and its calyx, enlarged.

apart. Plants in pots have a better chance, particularly against a southern sunny wall in a protected position, covered with a tent of plastic, and slit for access. Size of the plants may only reach about one foot or eighteen inches high and almost as wide, but this is only half the size of a plant in a perfect situation.

Kitchen: Use the leaves or whole young tops, chopped or whole. Basil may be a bit harsh for some people, so needs caution to begin with. For those who are fond of it, winter deprives them of one of the best herbs. **Soups:** Try it to taste, especially with Gazpacho. **Salads:** Mix with any salad, but particularly tomato with which it has a special affinity; or potato, rice and vegetable. **Vegetables:** Use with artichokes, beans, carrots, courgettes, cucumber, eggplant, mushrooms, onions, peas, green peppers, pumpkins, squash, tomatoes, ratatouille, casseroles. **Meat:** Use with beef, chicken, eel, fish, lamb, liver, pork, veal and sauces for same, particularly chicken and fish. Also mix into herb butters, pâtés and terrines (see p. 28). **Cheese:** Mix into cream and cottage cheeses. **Drinks:** Make tea from the leaves, or drop leaves into cool drinks. **Winter:** Use dried, deep-frozen or stored in oil. **Other uses:** Cook with millet, rice and red kidney beans. Use in sauces for pasta, the best being Pesto, a mixture of pounded Basil, nuts, garlic and cheese blended with olive oil and salt in a bowl or mortar, and when creamy added to any pasta dish.

BASIL: silhouette.

53

Bergamot (red) *Labiatae*
Monarda didyma

The young Bergamot can be most striking, with its pale tapering aromatic leaves held neatly in opposing pairs at intervals up its very pale square stem. The midribs of the leaves have a reddish tinge, and gradually the stems colour, the growing tips become almost purple, until finally they extend and symmetrical whorls of bright red flowers blossom to crown the plant. There are other colours in the blue-red range, and a white. The flowers show from July to September. Common names include Bee balm and Oswego tea.

Habitat and Cultivation: Brought to Europe from the eastern United States, where it grows in moist places near water from Michigan to Quebec, and can be found as far south as Georgia. Perennial, root runner. Dies down in winter, some young growth remaining to cover the roots in mild weather. Propagate by cuttings, root runners, root division in spring or autumn, or by seeds in spring. Place in a position of either semi-shade, or where the roots are shaded, and keep the plant moist. It grows to about two feet high and about as wide.

Kitchen: Use both the leaves and the flowers, but make sure that no small creatures lurk in those lovely long-necked flowers; tear the

BERGAMOT: silhouette.

55

leaves before using. **Salads:** Use in all kinds. **Meat:** Use in sausages, and sauces for pork and veal, or in sour cream added to both while cooking. **Cheese:** Mix with cream cheese, and cottage. **Drinks:** Tea from the leaves is known as Oswego tea. Flowers can be added, either to the brew, or into the cups when served. Cool drinks: leaves can be added to fruit or wine. **Winter:** Use deep-frozen or dried leaves.

Another Way to Hash Mutton: Cut your Mutton in little Bits, as thin as you can, strew a little Flour over it, have ready some Gravy, (enough for Sauce) wherin sweet Herbs, Onion, Pepper, and Salt, have been boil'd; strain it, put in your Meat, and a little Piece of Butter roll'd in Flour, and a little Salt, a Shalot cut fine, a few Capers, Samphire, and Gerkins, chopp'd fine, and a Blade of Mace: Toss all together for a Minute or two, have ready some Bread toasted thin, and cut into Sippets, lay it round the Dish, and pour in your Hash. Garnish your Dish with Pickles and Horse-radish. NOTE, Some love a Glass of Red Wine, or Walnut Pickle. You may put just what you will into a Hash.

Carbonaded Mutton: Get a Joint of Mutton, cut it into Steaks, and fry them in melted Lard, then stew them in Broth, with Salt, Pepper, and Cloves, a Bunch of Herbs, and Mushrooms; then flour it a little to thicken it. Garnish the Dish with Mushrooms and fry'd Bread, and serve it with Capers, and a little Lemon-juice.

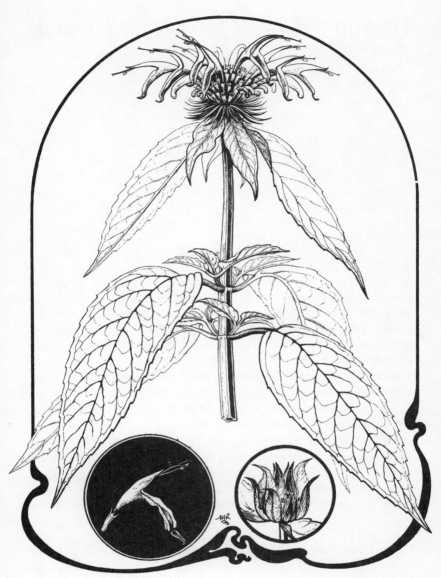

BERGAMOT: flowering top, slightly enlarged flower, and the tip before blooming.

Hyssop   *Labiatae*
Hyssopus officinalis

Hyssop is a bushy plant, with the ancient collapsing appearance of some *Labiatae*. Narrow pointed leaves grow in opposite pairs, on square, leaf-bearing stems which rise from the woody and rounded growth of the lower plant. To me the most fascinating aspect of this plant is its flowering system. Blue, pink or white blooms show from June to September, and appear to grow in one angle of the stem, formed by the opposite leaves. In fact, they form in neat groups above the leaves, but their stems twist the flowers around so that all face the same way from the same angle.

I can find very little to distinguish Hyssop from the Savories when neither is in flower, for early in the season all their leaves are roughly the same size. As the flowers appear, Hyssop has achieved leaves over an inch long, and the Savories put out new ones of only about half an inch in length. When they flower there is no longer any doubt. (See pp. 98, 99.)

Habitat and Cultivation: Southern Europe, Mediterranean. A sun lover, from dry stony ground or sandy soil. Hyssop is not found wild in the British Isles but is sometimes found in the northeastern United States and nearby Canada, on roadsides and in waste areas. Perennial, evergreen, but dropping some leaves in winter. Propagation is by seed in spring, or cuttings, or root division in spring or after flowering. The bush should be between one and two feet high and wide, and trimmed in spring or autumn.

Kitchen: Use flowers or leaves, and whole young tops, finely chopped or torn. Hyssop is a strongly flavoured herb, with the ability to make rich food easily digestible. Use it sparingly until familiar with the flavour. **Soups:** It is best with rich soups. **Salads:** Use flowers or leaves. **Meats:** Use in casseroles, sauces or stuffings, pâtés and terrines, especially with beef, duck, eel, fish, game, kidneys, lamb and pork. **Drinks:** Make tea from the leaves. **Winter:** Use the fresh plant, or deep-frozen, or stored in oil. **Other uses:** It is good with rice, lentils and fruit pies.

To Boil a Peacock. Flea off the Skin, but leave the Rump whole with the Pinions, then mince the Flesh raw with some Beef-sewet, season with Salt, Pepper, Nutmeg, and savoury Herbs shred small, and Yolks of Eggs raw; mingle with these some Marrow, the Bottoms of three Artichokes boil'd, Chesnuts, roasted and blanched, and Skirrets boil'd pretty small; then fill the Skin of the Peacock, and prick it up in the Back, set it to stew in a deep Dish in some strong Broth, White Wine, with Salt, large Mace, Marrow, Artichokes boiled and quartered, Chesnuts, Grapes, Barberries, Pears quarter'd, and some of the Meat made into Balls, cover it with another large Dish; when it is stew'd enough, serve it up on carv'd Sippets, broth it, and garnish with Slices of Lemon, and Lemon-peel whole, run it over with beaten Butter. Garnish the Dish with the Yolks of hard Eggs, Chesnuts, and Large Mace. (Skirret is a kind of parsnip.)

HYSSOP: flowering stem, and a leafy tip, also enlarged flowers. The lower left area shows a flattened flower group with dots above to indicate its actual arrangement, and a top and side view, then two simplified shapes which demonstrate the way the flower stalks turn the groups of flowers to one side.

HYSSOP: silhouette.

61

Lemon Balm
Melissa officinalis

Labiatae

The young plant sends up fine shoots at angles, with leaves sparsely but elegantly placed, but the mature plant is bushy and carries a thick cover of leaves, so that the square stems are almost hidden. Towards flowering time the tips extend and carry small white flowers like ragged nightgowns, in whorls at the leaf junctions. There are small white hairs on each calyx, and scattered along the tops of the leaf stalks, then more thickly across the thin ridge between leaf pairs. The leaves are veined so as to look wrinkled, and give off a lemon fragrance once bruised; like most plants the leaf size varies greatly with the situation. There is a variegated variety. Lemon Balm flowers from July to September.

Habitat and Cultivation: Southern Europe; naturalized in North America; occasionally found in hedgerows and woods. Perennial. Dies down in winter and may leave new emergent growth close to the ground in mild seasons. Propagate by seeds or cuttings or root division in spring or autumn, before frosts begin. It will grow in most soils, if not too dry or too wet, and grows to about twenty inches or more, and slightly wider.

Kitchen: Tear or chop the leaves, and use where a lemon tang is needed. **Soups:** Use chopped leaves in light soups e.g. chicken, and

Gazpacho (see p. 105). **Salads:** Use small pieces of leaf in all kinds, and in mayonnaise, sour cream and yoghurt. **Meat:** Add to chicken, pork, veal, casseroles and stuffing for poultry. Use in lemony sauces for chicken, fish, lamb, pork and veal; and as sweet herbs in the recipes below. **Cheese:** Mix into cream and cottage cheeses. **Drinks:** Make Melissa tea from the leaves, and drop leaves into cool drinks. **Winter:** It can be dried or deep-frozen. **Other uses:** Use in omelettes and soufflés. It is also good with fruit jellies, tarts and custards.

To Stew Pike Another Way: Clean well your Pike, and lard it with small Lardoons, then stew it in clarif'd Butter, Vinegar, Salt, Pepper, Nutmeg, and a Bunch of Sweet-Herbs, some Marjoram, and slic'd Lemon; make a Ragoo of Mushrooms, toss them up in Butter moistened with Fish-Broth; thicken your Sauce with some Flour, or Cullis, and when you dish up pour it upon your Pike. (For Cullis, see below.)

A Cullis of Roots: Take Parsnips, Carrots, Parsley-Roots, and Onions, and cut them in Slices; toss them up in a Stew-pan, then take about a Dozen and a half of blanch'd Almonds, and the Crumbs of two French Rolls soaked in good Fish-Broth, pound them together in a Mortar with your Roots; then boil all together, season them well as in other Cullises; then strain it, and use it for Soops of Cardoons, Chervil, Onions, Leeks, etc.

LEMON BALM: silhouette.

64

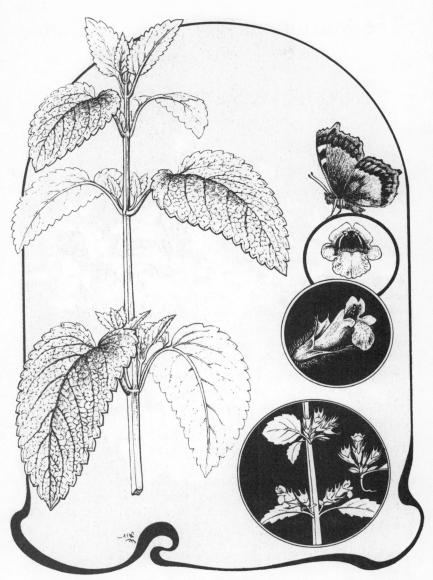

LEMON BALM: leaves before the stalk extends to flower, and in circle the finer flowering tip; also enlarged flowers.

The Marjorams   *Labiatae*

MARJORAM *Origanum vulgare*

There are wild and garden varieties of *Origanum vulgare,* with
green or golden foliage, on a bushy plant with square stems, oppo-
sitely branched and with opposite leaves. It is also known as Oregano
—a mild flavour compared with Mediterranean plants. The whole
plant is softly hairy, but more so just below leaf junctions, on the
flat faces not carrying leaves. The stems are sometimes quite purple.
Flowers of mauve or pink are carried in groups of three on three
stems which attach to another stem, itself part of a system of three.
They bloom from July to September. Another name is Joy of the
Mountain.

Habitat and Cultivation: Europe, scattered throughout England
and Ireland. Also found in the northeastern United States and
nearby Canada, on grasslands, especially chalky slopes in warm dry
areas. Perennial, dies down in winter. Propagate by seeds in spring,
root division or cuttings. Approximately eighteen inches high and
usually wider.

SWEET OR KNOTTED MARJORAM *Origanum marjorana*

Similar in many ways to *O. vulgare,* until the small squared buds
appear; presumably it is these which give the plant its name. Sweet

MARJORAM: showing silhouette, and typical Marjoram growth, with extending flower heads.

Marjoram, being an annual, may not achieve the size of the wild plant above, and will be quite distinctive as soon as the buds appear. Tips of small white petals seem to shelter between the formal shapes from August to September, by which time the "knots" will have extended into "plaits." To me the flavour of this Marjoram is far superior to that of other Marjorams; it has the true haunting aroma so good with tomatoes and pasta.

Habitat and Cultivation: Mediterranean. Usually treated as an annual as winter kills it off. Propagate by seed in spring. It requires a good light soil with plenty of sun, and will grow one or more feet high, and about half as wide.

POT MARJORAM *Origanum onites*

Again similar to *O. vulgare,* but more inclined to sprawl. It has white flowers from July to September.

Habitat and Cultivation: Hot dry ground near the Mediterranean. Perennial, dies down in winter. Propagate by the division of roots. Approximately one foot to eighteen inches high, and about two feet wide.

Kitchen: The flavours vary so much that it must depend upon the particular plant and the particular dish whether much or little Marjoram is used. Nothing is better than fresh Sweet Marjoram, and well-dried leaves of that plant are sometimes much better than fresh leaves of another variety, and anything, even no Marjoram at all, is better than the dried powder sometimes sold in memory of this delicious herb. Leaves should be torn, chopped or used whole. **Soups:** It is particularly good in vegetable. **Salads:** Use in all kinds. **Vegetables:** Use with beans, broccoli, brussels sprouts, carrots, cauliflower, courgettes, eggplant, mushrooms, onions, peas, spinach, stuffed peppers, summer squash, tomatoes, ratatouille and casseroles. **Meat:** Use with beef, chicken, fish, lamb, pork, rabbit, veal, sausages, stuffings, pâtés and terrines. **Cheese:** Mix with cream and cottage cheeses. **Winter:** Some plants will survive the winter under cloches, otherwise dried or frozen leaves are available. **Other uses:** It is good with many things, e.g. millet and rice, kidney beans, lentils, soybeans

MARJORAM: leaf stalk and flowering stem, with enlarged flowers and flower groupings of *O. vulgare*.

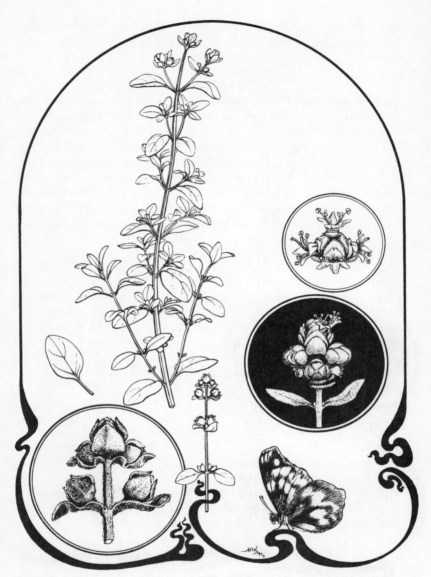

SWEET MARJORAM: showing leaf stalk with some flower buds, and a budded tip; also enlarged buds on the left, and more on the right with flowers squeezing through; and an enlarged flower.

and split peas, and pecans and walnuts. It can be added to sauces for lasagne, pizza and spaghetti, and baked in herb breads and scones.

To Stew a Rump of Beef: Having boiled it till it is more than half enough, take it up, and peel off the Skin: take Salt, Pepper, beaten Mace, grated Nugmeg, Parsley, Marjoram, Savoury, and Thyme shred, and stuff them in large Holes through the Fat; and lay the rest of the Seasoning all over the Top, and spread over it the Yolk of one or two Eggs to bind it on. Save the Gravy that runs out while you are stuffing it, and put to it a Pint of Claret, and some Vinegar; put it into a deep Pan, so fit for it, that the Liquor will fill it up to the Top; let it bake for two Hours, then put it into a Dish, and pour the Liquor it was baked in all over it.

Minced Sauce: Take some green Onions, Capers, Anchovies, and Parsley, cut small, each by itself upon a Plate, with a Clove of Garlick, and a Clove of Shalot; put all this into a Stew-pan together, with a few sweet Herbs, two Spoonfuls of Oil, as much of good Mustard, the Juice of a Lemon, with a little Cullis: Stir all well together, and you may use it with all Sorts of Fowls, and broil'd Meat, and with Roasted Meat, in a Saucer. (For Cullis, see p. 63.)

To Make Pottage de Santé: Put into a Pot good Broth, made of Buttock of Beef, Knuckle of Veal and Mutton, together with Capons or fat Pullets; season the Broth very well, then soak in some Crusts, while you are boiling Sorrel, Purslane, Chervil, etc., in another Pot, all cut very small; with these Herbs you may garnish your Pottage and Fowls, or you may strain them, so that you may put nothing in it but the Broth and good Gravy when you serve it up to Table.

A Stock for a Herb-soop: Get Chervil, Beets, Chards, Spinach, Sellery, Leeks, and such like Herbs, with two or three large Crusts of Bread, some Butter, a Bunch of sweet Herbs, and a little Salt;

71

put these, with a moderate Quantity of Water, into a Kettle, and boil them for an Hour and an Half, and strain out the Liquor through a Sieve, and it will be a good Stock for Soops, either of Asparagus Buds, Lettuce, or any other kind.

The Mints   *Labiatae*

Mints are very varied in leaf form, flavour and flowering spikes, but
all have square stems, white to purplish flowers, opposite leaves and
upright growth, generally unbranched unless the top leaves are
nipped out. Removal of flowering spikes will prevent the plants rac-
ing into bloom, and will keep the Mints green and leafy until frosts
come. Leaves vary from thin and slickly shiny to broad and woolly.
Flavour varies tremendously from plant to plant, and good Mints
may deteriorate after years in one place. There are far too many
varieties to mention more than a few, and cross-pollination succeeds
in producing new and changing varieties continually, making a
total count impossible.

Habitat and Cultivation: Europe, British Isles, the U.S.A., in moist
places and waste land by streams. Perennial, root runner. Dies down
in winter. Propagate by root division or runners, at any time of the
year. Mints will grow in almost any soil, but prefer partial shade in
deep rich and moist soil with good drainage. They will spread rap-
idly if not enclosed in some bottomless container, or it is possible to
check them by digging deeply around the area and pulling out
runners. Some will always escape, but they are controllable with
some effort, and if not, I doubt that it is possible to have too much

Mint. It is best not to plant different varieties close to one another, because apart from cross-pollination, Mints are very prone to Rust disease, which will affect a whole area, and the only cure is to dig up the plant and burn it, beginning again with healthy runners in another piece of ground.

SPEARMINT *Mentha viridis (spicata)*

Rare in the wild, but scattered throughout England, Scotland, Ireland, North America and Canada. Approximately eighteen inches high, and as broad as it is allowed. An even-coloured, almost hairless plant, leaves stalkless, finely serrated. Mauve flowers from August to September.

Kitchen: Use leaves and tops, whole or finely chopped or torn. Mint helps with digestion, breaking down fat and rich foods. **Soups:** Use in vegetable soup. **Salads:** Add to all kinds. **Vegetables:** Cook with beans, beetroot, cabbage, cauliflower, courgettes, leeks, peas, potatoes, spinach. **Meat:** As it aids digestion, mint sauce is useful as well as delicious with lamb. It is also good with cold chicken. Use it in sauces and as a garnish for beef, chicken, duck, fish, lamb and pork. **Cheese:** Use chopped leaves in cream and cottage cheeses. **Drinks:** Make tea for pleasure and for indigestion, and add leaves to other teas and cool drinks. **Winter:** Some will survive under cloches, otherwise dried leaves. **Other uses:** Use in omelettes and soufflés. It is delicious in a dish made with yoghurt, garlic crushed with salt and finely chopped cucumber.

PEPPERMINT *Mentha piperata*

The black variety is tinged browny-purple, particularly below the leaves; the white is untinged. It is found frequently in the south and west of England and over much of North America and Canada, and grows to approximately thirty or forty inches high. Almost hairless, stalked leaves are finely serrated. Perennial, root runner.

Kitchen: Check the flavour first. Leaves can be finely chopped. **Salads:** Use in all kinds. **Vegetables:** Cook with cabbage, carrots, cauliflower, peas, potatoes. **Meat:** Use as a garnish, or in jellies and

MINT: silhouette of Spearmint, typical growth pattern of the Mints.

MINT: flowering spike of Applemint (Bowles variety). Mint flowers in whorls about the stem above a leaf junction, so all Mints will be similar in that respect, though some heads are shorter and rounder than in this illustration, or more drawn out (see p. 79).

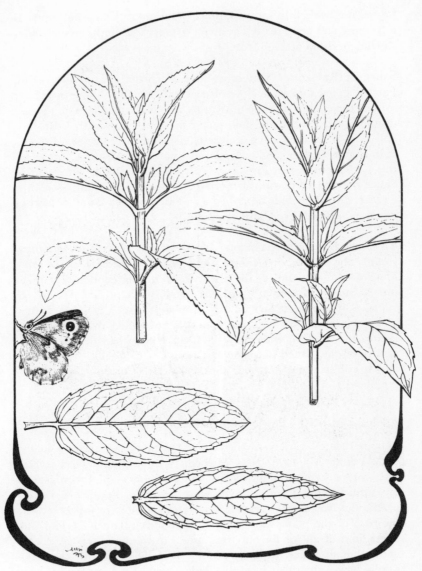

MINT: on the left, Peppermint, with its stalked leaves; on the right, Spearmint, no stalks and a slightly more noticeable rim of veins round the leaf.

sauces for beef, fish, lamb. **Drinks:** Tea made from the leaves is refreshing and good for indigestion. **Winter:** Use fresh, grown under cloches, or dried or deep-frozen.

Sauce in Ravigotte: You must take Terragon, Pimpernel, Mint, Parsley, green Onions, a little of each, blanch the Whole in boiling Water, then put it into cold Water; take it out again, and squeeze it, and cut it very small, then put it in a Stew-pan with a Rocambole bruis'd, a little Gravy, a little Cullis, and the Juice of a Lemon, Salt, beaten Pepper, an Anchovy cut small, and a little Oil; put all this a Moment over a Fire, and let it be well relish'd. This kind of Sauce may be used with all Sorts of roasted Meat, putting it in a Saucer. (Rocambole is described as a "kind of leek"; and a "sort of Spanish Garlick." For Cullis, see p. 63.)

To Dress Rabbit in Casserole: Divide the Rabbits into Quarters, you may lard them, or let them alone just as you please, shake some Flour over them, and fry them with Lard or Butter, then put them into a Stew-pan with a Quart of good Broth, a Glass of White Wine, a little Pepper and Salt, if wanted, a Bunch of sweet Herbs, and a Piece of Butter as big as a Walnut rolled in Flour; cover them close, and let them stew Half an Hour, then dish them up, and pour the Sauce over them. Garnish with Seville Orange cut into thin Slices and notched; the Peel that is cut out, lay between the Slices.

A P P L E M I N T , Bowles mint *Mentha rotundifolia*

A domesticated variety of the wild Applemint. Naturalized in the U.S.A. from Maine to New Mexico. A robust plant with thickly stiff square stems usually twenty to forty inches high, but sometimes much more. Largish leaves, whitely woolly, particularly underneath, and irregularly serrated; almost stalkless except for those near the base of the plant, which have slight stalks. This is perhaps the finest mint of all for flavour. It is useful in the same way as Spearmint, though I find it far superior especially raw, with the large woolly leaves shredded into all salads, Gazpacho, mayonnaise, sour cream, yoghurt, and on to dishes when serving. Pink flowers rise on long spikes from July to August (see p. 76).

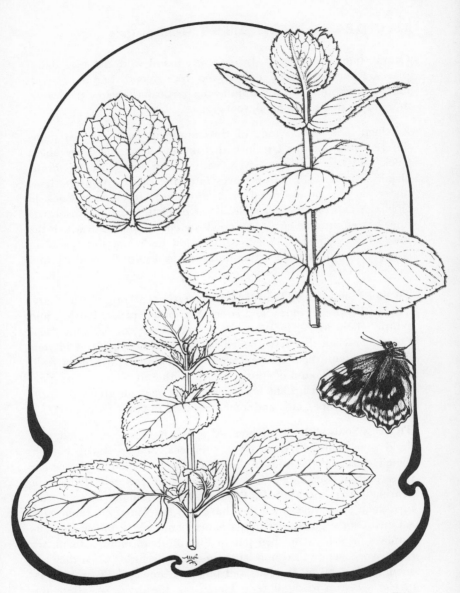

MINT: top, single leaf and tip of Applemint, Bowles variety; bottom, Eau de Cologne Mint.

EAU DE COLOGNE MINT *Mentha citrata*

Orange mint, lemon mint. Infrequently found wild, but likes damp places. Roundish leaves, stalked and very smooth and shiny with narrow serrations, and a purplish tint, particularly below the leaves, and purple stems. Perennial, root runner.

Kitchen: The special tang of this mint will lend itself to many different uses. **Salads:** Use in both fruit and vegetable. **Vegetables:** Cook with peas. **Cheese:** Mix with cream and cottage cheese. **Drinks:** Make tea, or drop leaves into cool drinks. **Winter:** Grow under cloches, or use dried or deep-frozen. **Other uses:** Cook in omelettes and soufflés, especially sweet omelettes made with orange juice beaten into the eggs. Also good is a cheese soufflé, to which the juice of an orange is added, with grated peel, and Orange Mint chopped both into the mixture and used as a garnish. Nutmeg and Coriander seed can also be added.

To Boil Flounders or Plaice: Boil sweet Herbs, Tops of Rosemary, Thyme, Winter Savoury, and sweet Marjoram, pick'd Parsley, and a little whole Mace, in White Wine and Water, of each an equal Quantity; when they have boiled for some Time, then put in your Flounders, skim them well, then put in the Crust of a French Roll, a Quarter of a Pound of Butter; season with Salt, Pepper, and Verjuice, and serve it up hot. (Verjuice is the acid juice of sour fruit, crab apples, grapes, etc., and sometimes used instead of vinegar.)

To Dress Soals with Cucumbers: After you have scaled, gutted, and dry'd your Soals, slit them down the Back, and fry them, cut off their Heads, and the Ends of their Tails, and set them to drain; cut three or four Cucumbers into Dice, lay them for two Hours in a Marinade of Vinegar, Salt, Pepper, and an Onion cut in Slices; turn them often, and when they have lain the Time, dry them with a Linen Cloth; put Butter into a Sauce-pan, melt it, put in the Cucumbers, brown them, then put in Fish-broth to moisten them, set them over a gentle Fire, and let them simmer a little; when they are enough, clear off all the Fat, and put in a brown Cullis to bind it, or else a Brown made of fry'd Flour; put the dry'd Soals into the Sauce-pan to the Cucumbers; let them simmer awhile, then dish them, pour the Ragoo over them, and serve them up.

Pennyroyal

Labiatae

Mentha pulegium

Upright Pennyroyal is a smooth plant reaching about two feet high, with opposite leaves appearing stalked, but in fact the leaf tapers to meet the square main stem, where a small stalked group of leaves arises from each junction. Mauve flowers mass in furry whorls from July to August.

Creeping Pennyroyal only rises a few inches from the ground, extending small shoots sideways to root at intervals and send up more shoots from the extensions. This form of growth is most suitable for places where it can creep from between stones in pavements, where it will be crushed to release its delightful aroma. Not everything enjoys this herb; it was once used to repel fleas. Its flowers are similar to those of Upright Pennyroyal.

Habitat and Cultivation: Central and southern Europe, British Isles. Not at all common, but found scattered in moist woody areas and marshes. Perennial, dies down in winter. Propagate by root division or runners, or by seed in spring. It needs protection from the sun, and likes a sheltered moist situation.

Kitchen: A herb to experiment with. Leaves are torn or used whole in stuffings and some rich sauces. A somewhat exotic aroma and rich minty flavour.

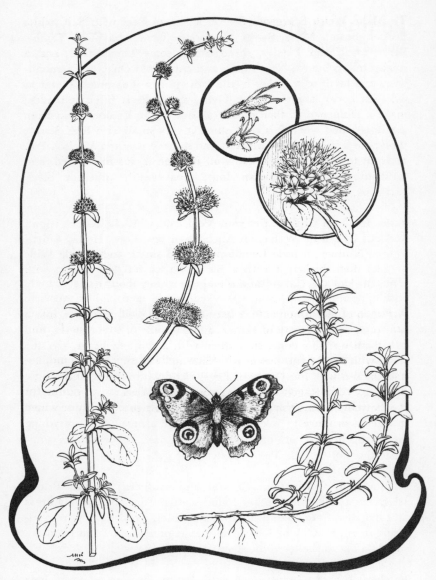

PENNYROYAL: Upright Pennyroyal on the left, showing two of the square stems, and beside them enlarged flowers in part of a whorl, and an enlarged single flower; on the right, Creeping Pennyroyal.

To Make Welsh Sturgeon: Season a Leg of Beef with Salt, white Pepper, beaten Mace, Sweet Marjoram, Winter Savoury, Thyme, Penny-royal, and Parsley, shred small; some Lemon-peel, and a small Onion; bone a Neat's foot, and cut it into Dice, or Diamond-wise, and lay it so together in the Pan; put to it as much Water as will just cover it, set it in an Oven, and bake it till it is tender; make a Dinner of it, then pick it all out of the Liquor, clean from the Bones, and when it is cold, shred it very small with Beef Sewet; then pound it in a Stone Mortar, and squeeze it into a Venison Pot, and put to it the Fat that came off it when it was first baked, and set it into a cool Oven for an Hour. (Neat was the word for "black cattle, ox, cow, bull.")

Sauce for Veal Cutlets: Fry your Veal, and when fry'd take it out, and put in a little Water, an Anchovy, a few sweet Herbs, a little Onion, Nutmeg, a little Lemon-peel shred small, and a little Wine or Ale, then thicken it with a Bit of Butter roll'd in Flour, with some Cockles and Capers, and then pour it over the Cutlets.

A Ragoo of Mushrooms: Pick and wash them well, put them into a Stewpan, with a Lump of Butter, and a Bunch of sweet Herbs, and toss them up; this done, stew them with a Dust of Flour, moisten them with Broth, and season with Salt and Pepper: Let all simmer, and thicken with four Yolks of Eggs, mix'd with Cream, and a little Nutmeg. Your Ragoo being of a good Taste, dish it up, putting at the Bottom of the Dish a Crust of Bread. (Ragoo: highly seasoned meat stew or sauce.)

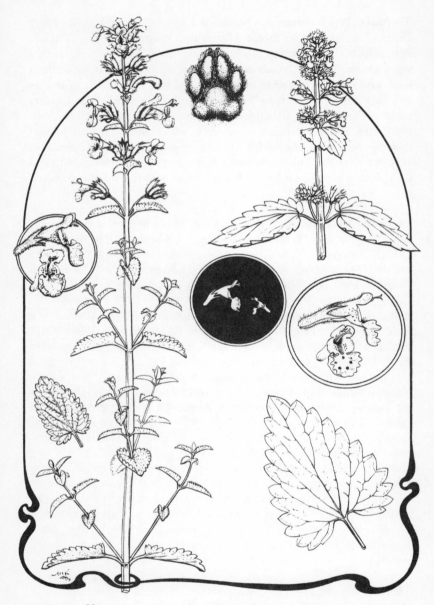

CATMINT: *Nepeta cataria* on the right, with its leaf below; on the left *Nepeta mussinii,* and its leaf beside it. In the circles are shown the flowers by their stalks, and in the centre the relative sizes of the flowers.

Catmint

Nepeta cataria

Labiatae

The two Catmints look very similar and in some situations almost identical until the flowers open. Both have the same number of slightly rounded indentations on the leaves, and are smoothly downy over the whole plant. *N. cataria* has a stem tinged with pink. It grows approximately three feet high, and bears very small white flowers spotted with red, in July to September. It is also called Catnip.

Habitat and Cultivation: Europe, central and southern England, the U.S.A. Unlike most mints, the Catmints like dry ground, and are found in waste areas, hedgerows, preferring chalk or gravel. Perennial, dies down in winter. Propagate by seed, or dividing plants, in spring. Cats are fascinated by Catmint and will sniff, pluck, roll about in and lie on the plants with the expected result to the growth unless some care is taken to protect it till maturity. A nice side story is that rats and mice are supposedly repelled by the plants, but some pet mice to whom I introduced leaves remained significantly unimpressed. Catmint sometimes dies away after flowering, so it is useful to have a younger plant ready to take its place.

Kitchen: Use leaves and young shoots. **Salads:** Use leaves, torn. **Meat:** include with seasonings, or use leaves rubbed into meat before roasting. **Drinks:** Tea can be made from leaves and dried flowering tops. **Winter:** Available dried. **For cats:** Small bunches tied and given to the cat will be promptly demolished by animals who have developed a passion for the smell; it seems to be a gradually acquired interest. A tidy way of indulging the cat is to sew dried leaves into a small piece of fine fabric.

Nepet mussinii

This domesticated variety is usually a smaller plant than *N. cataria,* but comparison with plants from different areas has shown there to be no apparent difference, one presumably being an older plant and from a more protected position was almost twice the usual size, and the leaves were identical. *N. mussinii* is perhaps rather more downy, which is unimportant unless both varieties are available for comparison. Its main stalks are pink towards the base. Mauve flowers dotted with red appear from June till early August.

Habitat and Cultivation: Perennial, dies down in winter. Propagate as above; the plant will probably grow to about eighteen inches to two feet high. Because it is a weaker plant than wild Catmint, it is best to leave some growth around the roots rather than cut down the dead growth. This variety is inclined to collapse if exposed to much wind, and may not grow at all in some exposed places. The way to find the best place is to put a potted plant in different places until it has decided where it is happy; if conditions are not right it will surely let you know, but will recover with good grace if moved soon enough.

Rosemary
Rosmarinus officinalis

Labiatae

Rosemary can look both on the point of collapse and full of life, as the main branches have a sprawling habit, while all the new growth stretches to the sky. Shreddy grey-beige bark covers the lower plant, on which shoots appear almost at random, and on these shoots are leaves placed opposite each other, often on side shoots again placed opposite. The leaves appear rigid, but are softly leathery, dark blue-green on top with sides curling down to turn inwards over the spongy white undersurface. The flowers are a delicate pale blue, lightly marked with purple on the lower lip. There are varieties of Rosemary, including a tiny creeping plant, only inches high. They flower from May to June, and sometimes in autumn. It is also called Dew of the Sea.

Habitat and Cultivation: Mediterranean, not wild in the British Isles or the U.S.A. It likes sheltered spots in dry, rather poor soil, preferring chalk, where it produces a smaller but more aromatic plant. Perennial, evergreen. Rosemary may be killed in a bad winter. It does best when grown against a south-facing wall, where it can catch the sun and avoid the wind. Propagation can be by seed, but is far easier if heeled cuttings are taken in spring, or after the parent plant has flowered. Or by layering during summer

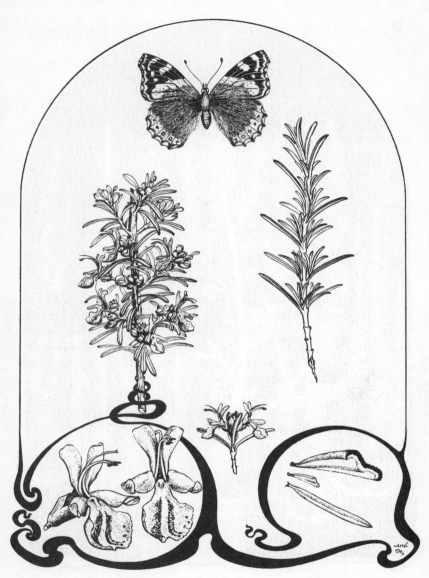

ROSEMARY: shows middle part only of a flowering stem (all the upper branches carry flowers) and enlarged flowers, leaf tip, flowering tip, and leaf with enlargement.

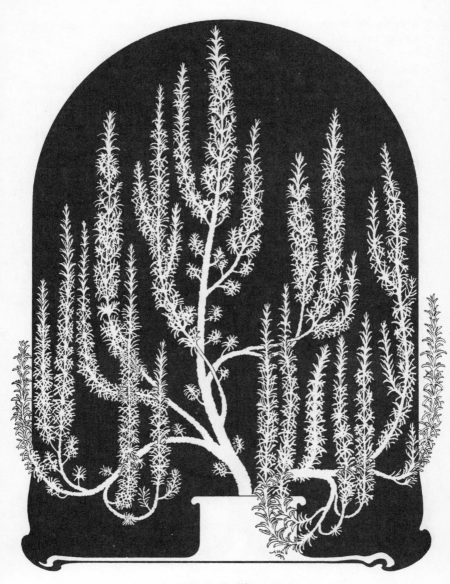

ROSEMARY: silhouette.

growth. Rosemary can be five feet high, or much more, and may be almost as broad.

Kitchen: Use leaves and whole young tops, finely chopped, or the whole sprig where it can impart flavour but be removed after cooking, otherwise it can make a very strong-tasting woody mouthful. Rosemary will overpower other flavours if recklessly used, but it is one of the best aromatic herbs. Soups: Use in both meat and vegetable. Salads: Use leaves chopped very fine and used sparingly. Vegetables: Use with beans, cauliflower, cucumber, mushrooms, parsnips, peas, baked potatoes (particularly if cooked in bacon fat), and spinach. Meat: Use with roast beef, chicken (especially tucked into the crevices) duck, fish, lamb, pork, veal and shellfish, and marinades for all. A good recipe is chicken, covered with bacon and orange slices, stuffed with oranges and cloves, and served with orange sauce. Also pâtés, potted meats and terrines. Cheese: Use with cream and cottage cheese. Drinks: Make tea, particularly brewed with orange peel and served with Mint. For colds, a soothing tea can be made with half a teaspoon of ground ginger and a spoonful of honey. Winter: Rosemary can be dried, but then the leaves become needle-like, and are only suitable for long cooking unless tied in muslin. The bush retains its leaves all year. Other uses: Use with scrambled eggs and omelettes. Cook with rice, lentils, sauces for pasta and in herb breads.

To Boil a Leg of Mutton: You must lard your Mutton with Lemon-peel and Beetroot, and boil it as usual: For Sauce, take strong Broth and White Wine, Gravy, Oysters, Anchovies, an Onion, a Faggot of Herbs, Pepper, Salt, and Mace, and a Piece of Butter roll'd up in Flour.

Sage

Salvia officinalis

Labiatae

There are several varieties of Sage, which is confusing, but when narrowed down to culinary plants they seem to be too similar to warrant more than two drawings. Broad-leaved Sage, which one would think was Common Sage, does not apparently flower in England, and must be grown from cuttings (as are most sages). Narrow-leaved Sage does flower, and from this presumably is derived a broad-leaved variety. Then there are two very pretty sages. The first, Red or Purple Sage, can have very large leaves, the new ones quite purple, paler below. Older leaves become green, but have purple veining, even more striking on the undersurface; the stem and leaf stalks are the same colour. The other is Golden Variegated, deep green in the centre of the leaves, and pale gold in irregular marking on the outer edges.

Common Sage is another collapsing yet erect-looking *Labiatae*. Sage forms a bush with woody stems and haphazard branching which extends into pale squared stems with reddish corners, carrying thick textured leaves in opposite pairs. These leaves release a strong aroma when bruised. Purple flowers appear in May till July.

Habitat and Cultivation: Northern Mediterranean. Sometimes found wild in the U.S.A., it likes dry places, especially on chalkland near the sea. Perennial, evergreen, though it does drop some leaves during winter. Propagate by cuttings, or layering during the growing season, or by seed in spring into a sunny place. Mature plants become straggly, though they will bush out if kept trimmed back; removal of flowering stems leaves a bush of fresh branches and new growth. Flowers on one bush may vary from blue to pink. Size will be up to about three feet high, and about as wide.

Kitchen: Leaves, torn or chopped. Sage is a very useful herb in helping with the digestion of rich food, hence its use in stuffings and with legumes. It has a strong flavour which when fresh and properly used can be very pleasant, but when dried can degenerate, and some powdered Sage on sale is simply a rather ominously pungent dust. Use only a leaf or two at first. **Soups:** It is good in vegetable. **Vegetables:** Use with beetroot, carrots, beans, eggplant, onions, peas, potatoes, spinach and tomatoes. **Meat:** Rub into, or chop fine and cook with beef, chicken, duck, eel, fish, goose, hare, lamb, liver, pork, rabbit, turkey, veal and venison. Also use in meat loaves, pâtés, sausages, terrines, etc. **Cheese:** Use in cream cheese or with cheddar. **Drinks:** Make tea from the leaves (see Medicinal Uses). **Winter:** It is available dried, deep-frozen, or fresh from the plant. **Other uses:** Cook with chick peas, kidney beans, soybeans, split peas and other pulses; also almonds, pecans and walnuts.

To Marinate Salmon to Be Eaten Either Hot or Cold: Take a Salmon, cut it into Joles and Rands, and fry them in Sallad Oil, or clarified Butter, then set them by, then put into a Pipkin as much Claret and Wine Vinegar as will be sufficient to cover them; put in a Faggot of sweet Herbs, as Rosemary, Thyme, Sweet Marjoram, Winter-Savoury, Parsley, Sage, Sorrel, and Bay Leaves, Salt, gross Pepper, Nutmeg, and Ginger sliced, large Mace and Cloves, boil all these well together; lay your Salmon into a Pan, and all being cold, pour this Liquor over it, lay on sliced Lemons and Lemon-peel, and cover it up close; and you may either serve it hot or cold, with the same Liquor it was soused in, with Spices, Herbs, and Lemons on it.

To Souse Soals: Scotch your Soals on the white Side thick, but not deep; boil them in White Wine, Wine Vinegar, Salt, sliced Ginger, Cloves, and Mace, just as much as will cover them; when your Liq-

SAGE: silhouette.

93

SAGE: detail with enlarged flower.

uor boils put in your Soals, then put in sliced Onions, Winter-Savoury, sweet Marjoram, Rosemary, Sage, Thyme, and Parsley; when they are boiled enough set them by to cool.

To Fry Roaches: Gut, scale, and wash them in Salt and Water, and wipe them clean with a Napkin; then flour them, and fry them in fresh Butter till they are brown and crisp; then take them out, and lay them in a heated Dish; set them before the Fire to keep; pour off the Butter you fry'd them in; then in other Butter fry Sage and Parsley crisp, and lay them on your Roaches. In the mean Time, let some Butter be beaten up, with a few Spoonfuls of scalding hot Water, in which Anchovy has been dissolved, and pour this Sauce over your Roaches: Garnish the Dish with Parsley and Strawberry-leaves, and serve it up.

To Marinate Neat's Tongues: Boil them, blanch them, lard them, if you please, put them in a Vessel; make a Pickle of Nutmegs and Ginger slic'd, large Mace, whole Cloves, a Bunch of sweet Herbs, Parsley, sweet Marjoram, Rosemary, Thyme, Winter-savoury, Sage, and Bay-leaves; boil these in as much Wine Vinegar and White Wine as will fill the Vessel you put your Tongues into; put in some Salt and slic'd Lemons; when they are cold close them up for use, serve them with some of the Liquor, Spices, Herbs, and Sallad Oil, and Slices of Lemon. (Neat, see p. 83.)

To Boil a Leg of Veal and Bacon: Lard your Leg of Veal all over with pretty large Lardoons of Bacon, and Lemon-peel, boil it with a Piece of middling Bacon; when the Bacon is enough cut it into Slices, season them with dry Sage and Pepper mix'd together. Dish the Veal, lay the Bacon round it, strew it over with Parsley, and serve it with green Sauce in Saucers; which green Sauce you must make as follows: Beat two or three Handfuls of Sorrel in a Mortar, with a Couple of Pippins quarter'd, and put to it Vinegar and Sugar. Or take a Couple of Handfuls of Sorrel, pound it in a Mortar, squeeze out the Juice, and put it in a Pipkin, with a little drawn Butter and Sugar, and grated Nutmeg. Warm it, and pour it on your Veal and Bacon.

Another Sauce for Boiled Chickens or Lamb: Take a little White Wine and a Pint of Claret, a few Sprigs of sweet Herbs, a little whole Pepper, and Mace, three Slices of Lemon; let it stew a little; then put in a little Parsley and Spinach boil'd green, and chopp'd a little; then beat it up thick with six Ounces of fresh Butter, and pour it over the Meat, and serve it. Garnish it with Lemon sliced, and Barberries, Grapes, and Gooseberries scalded, in their Season.

The Savories   *Labiatae*

SUMMER SAVORY *Satureia hortensis*

Summer Savory has upright, square stems, opposite leaves and branches. The leaves are V-shaped at first, older ones flatten and droop. The plant has a pinkish stem, covered with fine short white hairs. Pale mauve flowers appear from August to September.

Habitat and Cultivation: Mediterranean. Not wild in the British Isles. Sometimes found in fields and waste places in the northeastern United States and nearby Canada. It likes the sun, and rich, light soil, growing to approximately one foot high and wide. Annual. Propagate by seed in early spring, sow in a sunny position, leaving plants about one foot apart.

WINTER SAVORY *Satureia montana*

A small shrubby plant, sharing the habit of woody stemmed *Labiatae* by having barked and ancient looking main growth, from which new shoots stretch upwards on square stems, covered with fine short hairs, and carrying pointed, shiny opposite leaves. The flowers are white, pink, or pale blue-purple, and appear to almost cover the plant from July till September.

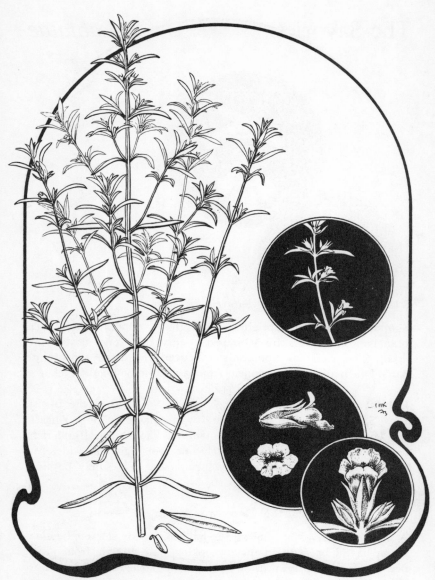

SUMMER SAVORY: showing upright growth, leaves and flowering stem, with enlarged flowers.

WINTER SAVORY: with sprawling yet upright growth, leaves, an enlarged flowering group and flowers. The whole plant is very similar to Hyssop (pp.60, 61).

Habitat and Cultivation: Mediterranean. Not wild in the British Isles or the U.S.A. Dry, poor soil in the sun is necessary. Perennial, evergreen. Propagate by seed in spring, by cuttings, or layering during the growing season. Too much moisture will make more growth, but weakens the plant so that it may be killed by frosts. Cut back in autumn. The bush will be about twelve to twenty inches high and wide.

Kitchen: Both Savories have similar uses, and as the plants will vary in flavour at different times it is as well to taste a leaf before using. Summer Savory is to my taste peppery and aromatic, while Winter is peppery with a dash of lemon. Both help with digestion and flatulence, making them particularly useful with cucumber and all types of beans, whose flavour they also encourage. Use leaves or young tops chopped or torn. **Soups:** Good in thick soups particularly those using beans or peas. **Vegetables:** Use with artichokes, asparagus, all beans, brussels sprouts, cabbage, marrow, peas, potatoes, sauerkraut, spinach and turnips. **Meat:** Cook with beef, chicken, duck, eel, fish, ham, lamb, pork, rabbit, turkey, veal, venison and sauces for all. Also use in meat loaves, pâtés, sausages, stuffings, terrines. **Cheese:** Use in cream cheese. **Drinks:** Make tea with leaves. **Winter:** Both can be dried or frozen. Winter Savory keeps its leaves all winter. **Other uses:** Use in omelettes, and with lentils, soybeans, all beans, and rice.

To Make Force-meat Ball: Get a Pound of Veal, and the same Weight of Beef-sewet, and a Bit of Bacon, shred all together; beat it in a Mortar very fine; then season it with sweet Herbs, Pepper, Salt, Cloves, Mace and Nutmegs; and when you roll it up to Fry, add the Yolks of two or three Eggs to bind it. You may add Oysters, or Marrow, at an Entertainment.

Thyme

Thymus vulgaris

Labiatae

Common Thyme (*T. vulgaris*) is only one of the species of Thyme, some of which are bushy, some creeping and diminutive. All have the peculiar fragrance, some combined with a strong lemon scent and flavour, and one, *Herba barona,* reminds me of spices. *Vulgaris* has the usual collapsing air combined with upward stretching new growth of the family, and its stem gives way from rough wood to tender square shoot, carrying opposite leaves whose edges curl round to the paler under-leaf. The upper surfaces are marked with small indentations, and there is almost no indication of veins. Pink flowers bloom from May to July.

Habitat and Cultivation: Southern Europe, Mediterranean. Light, dry, chalky soil, in a warm windless spot. It is not wild in the British Isles or the U.S.A., though related to the wild variety. Perennial, evergreen. Propagate by seed, or preferably by cuttings or root divisions in spring or autumn, or by layering, building soil up about the mature bush and pinning down the branches. Thyme can straggle and fall about, so benefits from some cutting back in autumn. A mature plant will reach about one foot high and may be almost twice as wide.

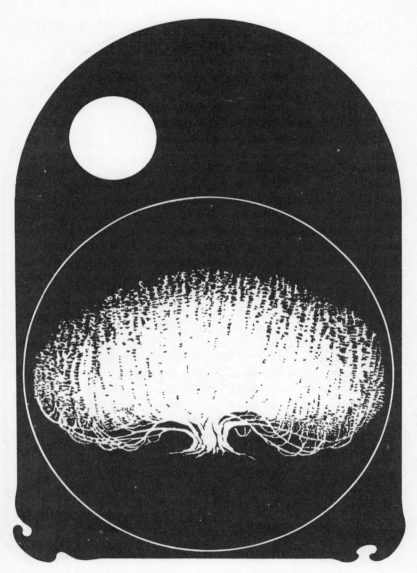

THYME: silhouette of *vulgaris,* a typical Thyme growth.

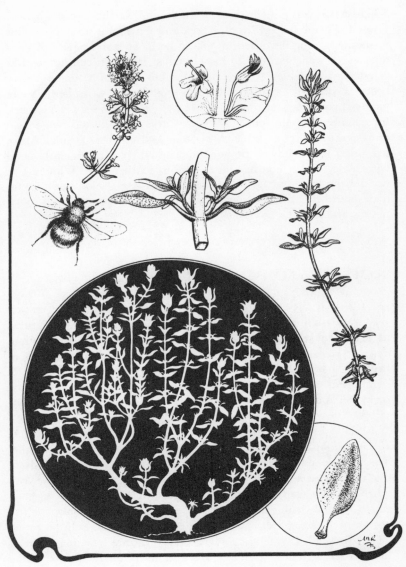

THYME: young plant of the same, with enlarged flower, branching, and leaf, also flowering and leaf tops.

Kitchen: Leaves, pulled from the stalk, and, in the larger Thymes, bruised. Thyme helps with digestion, and Thymol is antiseptic. This is another strong-flavoured, aromatic herb. **Soups:** As part of bouquet garni, add sparingly to taste. **Salads:** It is particularly good in coleslaw. **Vegetables:** Use with asparagus, eggplant, green beans, beets, cabbage, carrots, courgettes, mushrooms, onions, sweet peppers, potatoes and tomatoes. **Meat:** Use with beef, chicken, eel, fish, lamb, mussels, pork, scallops, turkey, veal, and wine and tomato sauces for the same. Also pâtés and terrines. **Drinks:** Make tea, using rather less of the herb than usual. It is particularly good with honey and lemon or orange peel to soothe colds. **Winter:** Use dried, deep-frozen or from the bush. **Other uses:** Cook in omelettes and pancakes, with rice, red kidney beans, soybeans, split peas, pecans, walnuts and sauces for pasta.

SOME THYME VARIETIES

HERBA BARONA *Herba barona* has diminutive leaves on very weak trailing stems; even though the plant is prostrate, it turns its leaves to keep a flat side to the sun. A particularly delicious Thyme, at one time used with such splendid dishes as Baron of Beef. It has a more exotic flavour than most Thymes, subtly reminiscent of spices and oil. A native of Corsica, from dry sandy, rocky soil, and chalk. Deep mauve flowers cover it in June and July.

WILD THYME The British Isles has three wild Thymes, one, *T. serpyllum,* being extremely rare, and found only in East Anglia. The European *T. serpyllum* has escaped into fields and woods of the northeastern United States and adjacent Canada. The two other varieties can usually be distinguished by the lines of hairs which run down the stems. For the purposes of this book it is not necessary to distinguish between the two, as they can both be eaten. They are Wild Thyme, *Thymus drucei,* prostrate creeping plant of dry grasslands, and on chalky areas in the south; flowering from June to August. The other is Large Wild Thyme, more variable in size but less creeping in most cases, depending on the situation, found mostly on chalk in the south of England.

THYMUS SERPYLLUM This is a domesticated variety, with minute leaves in rosettes on a quite prostrate plant, with masses of white or red flowers from May to July.

THYMUS CITRIODES The variegated variety seems to have the greatest tang of lemon, and is a more spectacular plant, with leaf centres of green edged with yellow, on purple stalks, the leaves showing a deep red flush from below. Lemon scent drifts through the air after only brushing the plant. Both Thymes have mauve flowers from late May till August.

BROAD-LEAVED THYME It has quite wide leaves; otherwise it is much like *T. vulgaris,* with mauve flowers in July and August.

A Good Savoury Broth for Mornings: Make very good Broth with some Lean of Veal, Beef, and Mutton, and with a Brawny Hen, or young Cock; after it is skimm'd, put in an Onion quarter'd, and, if you like it, a Clove of Garlick, a little Parsley, a Sprig of Thyme, as much Mint, a little Balm, some Coriander Seed bruised, and a very little Saffron, a little Salt, Pepper, and a Clove, when all the Substance is boiled out of the Meat, and the Broth very good, you may drink it so, or pour a little of it upon toasted sliced Bread, and stew it till the Bread has soak'd up all that Broth, then add a little more, and stew; so adding Broth by little and little, that the Bread may imbibe it and swell; wheras, if you drown it at once, the Bread will not swell, and grow like a Jelly; and thus you will have a good Pottage: You may add Cabbage, or Leeks, or Endive, or Parsley-Roots, in the due Time, before the Broth has ended boiling, and Time enough for them to become tender. In the Summer you may put in Lettuce, Sorrel, Purslane, Borrage, and Bugloss, or what other Pot-Herbs you like; but green Herbs take away the Strength and Cream of the Pottage.

To Hash a Shoulder of Mutton: Your Shoulder being half roasted, cut it in very thin Slices, then take a Glass of Claret, a Blade of Mace, two Anchovies, a few Capers, a Shalot, Salt, a Sprig of Thyme, Savoury, and Lemon-peel; let it stand cover'd for half an

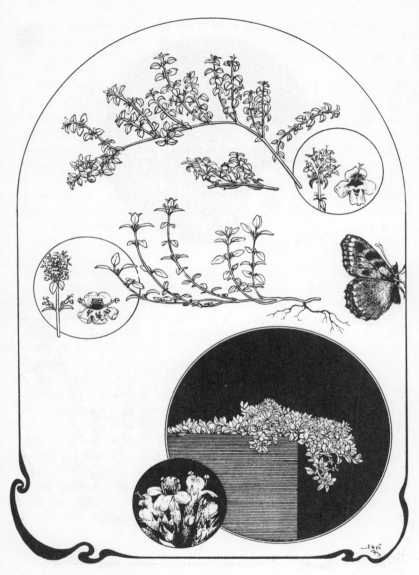

THYME: top left, *Herba barona,* flower and spike; centre, creeping specimen of Large Wild Thyme; bottom, *Thymus serpyllum,* showing creeping
habit and enlarged flowers.

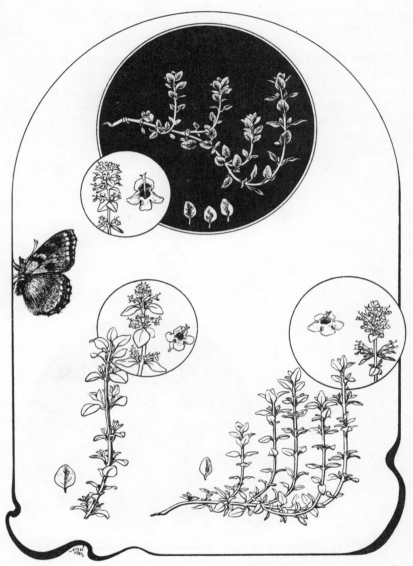

THYME: top, variegated Lemon Thyme with leaves, flowering spike and enlarged flower; lower right, ordinary Lemon Thyme; lower left, Broad-leaved Thyme.

Hour in an Oven; and when enough, shake over it some Capers, and serve it up.

Mutton Grilled with Capers: Boil a large Breast of Mutton tender, and after you have carbonaded it all over, season it with Pepper and Salt; then wash it over with Yolks of Eggs, Crumbs of Bread, a little Thyme chopp'd and Parsley, then broil it gently. For Sauce take Butter, Gravy, Capers, Shalots, and Mangoes, or Mushrooms cut small. (Carbonade, "meat cut across to be broiled, cut or hack.")

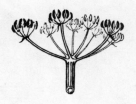

UMBELLIFERAE

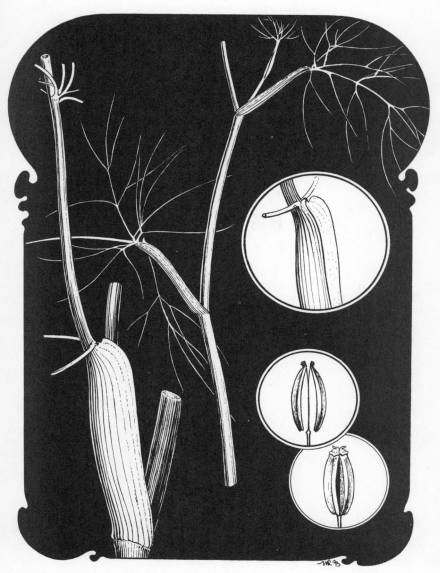

UMBELLIFERAE: the sheathing leaf bases of a Fennel plant, fronds of the leaf having been removed from the stalk on the left. Also two dried seeds of Lovage, one showing the way two carpels lift sideways before dropping.

Umbelliferae

It has not been practicable to do silhouette drawings for the plants in the following section, nor is there one plant which can be called typical. But the family is vast, and once identified certain characteristics will be evident. The name arises, obviously, from the umbrella shape of the flowering heads, usually white, varieties of which can be seen in profusion along the roadsides in spring and summer. This is the chief feature for recognition, though a few members have such cleverly arranged umbels as to make the exception. (For example, Sea-Holly.)

The leaves divide and sub-divide in shapes from delicate fern to ragged green cloth, and the stems have bases which are sheathed to wrap the main stem. These sheaths sometimes continue away from the stem as a kind of open gutter, with small leaflets at their tip, and some flowering stems rise from inside. The accepted difficulties of recognising many of the plants within the family have resulted in close examination of the seeds, and it is these which will often provide the safest method of identification; hence descriptions of them are usually available in reference books. Mention is not always made, however, that fresh seeds are smoother and fuller than dried, and that a wrinkled and readily recognisable seed will sometimes have taken so long to ripen that the plant will be in tatters of decay below it. Luckily many of the umbelliferous herbs used for culinary or medical purposes can be safely identified without relying on seed identification, as I have tried to show in the following pages.

Angelica   *Umbelliferae*
Angelica archangelica

There are two European Angelicas, *A. archangelica,* and *A. sylvestris,* which is found wild, and is very similar to Garden Angelica, though the flavour is not so subtle. There are also some American varieties. The plant can grow very tall, its leaves and stalk can be immense. In its first year or two it will simply send out large leaves on smooth "bloomed" stalks, which flop over somewhat with their own weight, and entirely if they lack water. The main stalk is wrapped at intervals with the sheathing leaf bases, uppermost of which shelter flowering stems, and may be quite small. Umbels are almost round and can be six to eight inches across, covered with greenish white flowers from May to June. Seeds are flat and disclike, even before separating.

Habitat and Cultivation: Garden Angelica comes from the cooler parts of Europe, and is only rarely found wild in the British Isles or the U.S.A. It grows in shady places with rich damp soil. Wild Angelica is common in the British Isles and can be found in the northeastern United States and nearby Canada, by riverbanks and moist shady places. Garden Angelica is treated as a biennial, as it dies after flowering, but in some conditions it may not flower for some years, so it is also a perennial. It dies down in winter. Propa-

ANGELICA: drawn to half scale (see hen's egg). Leaves can be over two feet long, flower heads eight inches. Also shown are an enlarged flower with dropped stamens, and a seed, further enlarged.

gate by seeds, which should be sown as soon as they ripen in August or September. Best of all, obtain a young plant which will eventually self-sow, ensuring continuing plants. Height up to eight feet and half as wide at least.

Kitchen: Use the leaves and young stems as a vegetable, either raw or steamed or boiled, with plain or herb butter. The real benefit of Angelica is in its sweetness, which will reduce the tartness of some cooked fruits; for example, some stems or roots can be boiled with rhubarb. Leaf tips can flavour jams and jellies, and young stems can be candied. This is done by boiling pieces about four inches long, for about twenty minutes, peeling the stems and slicing them, then cooking again, this time with some sugar added to the water. Let the stems lie for two days after straining, with a pound of sugar to a pound of stalks, in a bowl or dish. Using the strained syrup, and adding a little more sugar, bring the liquid to the boil, drop in the stalks and boil for another twenty minutes. Strain off, cool, and store. **Drinks:** Make tea from the leaves. **Winter:** Use candied stalks.

To Make Pottage Without the Sight of Herbs: Mince several Sorts of sweet Herbs very fine, Spinach, Scallions, Parsley, Marygold Flowers, Succory, Strawberry and Violet leaves, stamp them with Oatmeal in a Bowl or Mortar; then strain them with some of your Broth, boil your Oatmeal and Herbs, with Mutton, season with Salt, etc.; when all is enough, serve it up with Sippets.

Eggs with Rose Water: Let your Eggs be temper'd with Rose-water, Salt, beaten Cinnamon, Maccaroon, and Lemon-peel, boil them with clarify'd Butter in a Pan over a gentle Fire; when they are enough, ice them over with Sugar and Orange-flower, or Rosewater; and, when you serve them up, put some lemon juice and the Kernals of Pomegranates to them.

ANISE: showing progressive changes in leaf shape, also umbel, an enlarged flower and seed (dried).

Anise   *Umbelliferae*
Pimpinella anisum

Anise shows at first as the two long narrow leaves typical of shoot-
ing umbellifers, then the progression of shapes begins, first with an
almost round leaf, slightly indented in two places, giving way gradually to increasingly finely cut shapes till the final is almost feathery.
The umbels have white flowers in July.

Habitat and Cultivation: Native of the Mediterranean, where it is
much used in drinks; escaped in Massachusetts. Annual, propagate
by seed in spring, in a sunny place. The plants are not robust, but
will reach eighteen inches or more, and need to be spaced about ten
inches apart.

Kitchen: Valued as a relief for flatulence, as well as its haunting
flavour. Use seeds and leaves. **Soups:** It is good in rich creamy
soups. **Salads:** Use leaves and seeds in all kinds, but taste them first!
Meat: Scatter a few seeds onto grilled fish, pork and veal, and into
apple sauce. Use leaves as a garnish, or in curries and pickles.
Drinks: Crush seeds and make into a soothing tea. **Winter:** Use
dried seeds. **Other uses:** Scatter into omelettes, or cook in herb
bread, spiced cake and puddings.

To Stew a Fillet of Beef in the Italian Fashion: Take the Skins and Sinews from a Fillet of Beef, put it into a Bowl with White Wine, crush it in and wash it well; then strew upon it a little Pepper, and a Powder called the Italian Tamara, (which is made of one Ounce of Coriander-seed, half an Ounce of Fennel-seed, half an Ounce of Anniseed, an Ounce of Cinnamon, and an Ounce of Cloves, beaten into a gross Powder, with a little Powder of Winter-savoury; these all kept in a Glass Vial) and as much Salt as will season it; mingle them all well together, and put as much White Wine as will cover it; put a Board on it to keep it down, and let it lie in steep for two Nights and a Day; then take it out, and put it into a Stew-pan, with some good Broth that is Salt, but none of the Pickle; put in whole Cloves, and Mace, cover it close, let it stew till it is tender, then serve it with as much of the Broth as will cover it.

To Make Pottage the Italian Way: Boil green Peas in some strong Broth, with interlarded Bacon cut into Slices; when the Peas are boiled, put to them Pepper, Anniseeds, and chopp'd Parsley, and strain some of the Peas to thicken the Broth; let it have a Walm or two, and serve it on Sippets with boil'd Chickens, Pigeons, Lamb's Head, Duck, or any Fowl; you may, if you please, thicken the Broth with Eggs.

Olives of Veal: Wash ten or twelve Scotch Collops with Batter of Eggs, and season them; then lay over them a little Forc'd-meat, roll them up, and roast them: Make for them a Ragoo, and garnish the Dish with slic'd Orange. (Walm, a period of boiling; Collop, a small slice of meat; Ragoo, highly seasoned stewed meat or sauce.)

Caraway

Carum carvi

Umbelliferae

In its first year Caraway has a bushy growth with many leaves rising from the ground. It seeds in its second year, in umbels which carry white flowers in June.

Habitat and Cultivation: Europe, temperate Asia, India and north Africa. Rarely found wild in the British Isles, but common in parts of the U.S.A., in waste areas and semi-shade. Biennial. Dies down in winter. Propagate by seeds in spring or autumn. Caraway may grow from one to three feet high.

Kitchen: Young leaves are used: peeled roots, and seeds, crushed or whole. Most umbellifers help with digestion, and Caraway is one of these. **Soups:** Use young leaves as a garnish. **Salads:** Use young leaves, torn or chopped, and seeds, particularly with coleslaw. **Vegetables:** Use to flavour brussels sprouts, cabbage, cauliflower, celery, potatoes, turnips. As a vegetable Caraway roots, when not too old, can be steamed or boiled. **Meat:** Seeds can be sprinkled on roast beef, chicken, fish and lamb. Also in goulash Caraway and Oregano complement the Paprika if the former is sparingly used. **Cheese:** Use in cream and cottage cheeses. **Drinks:** Make tea with the seeds. It is useful for flatulence if used with equal quantities of Anise and

Fennel. **Winter:** Seeds are available. **Other uses:** Seeds can be cooked or served separately at table with pies or baked apples. They can be cooked with rice, and nut loaf, and also with bread and cakes, either in the mixture or on the surface.

To Dress Red Herrings with Cabbage: Boil your Cabbage tender, then put it into a Saucepan, and chop it with a Spoon; put in a good Piece of Butter, let it stew, stirring it lest it should burn: Take some Red Herrings and split them open, and toast them before the Fire till they are hot through. Lay the Cabbage in a Dish, and lay the Herrings on it, and send it hot to Table. Or you may pick your Herrings from the Bones, and throw the Meat over your Cabbage: Hold the hot Salamander over the Dish a little, and serve away quick. (Salamander is a kitchen utensil.)

To Roast a Leg of Mutton: Pare off all the Skin as thin as you can, then lard it with fat Bacon, and put it down to the Fire, when it is half roasted, cut off three or four thin Slices, and mince it with some sweet Herbs; then put it into a Sauce-pan, with a Ladleful of Broth, half a Pint of Red Wine, a little beaten Ginger, a Piece of Butter, two spoonfuls of Verjuice or Vinegar, some Pepper, a few Capers, and the Yolks of two hard Eggs chopp'd small; let 'em all stew a-while, and when your Leg of Mutton is enough, dish it up, and pour this Sauce over it.

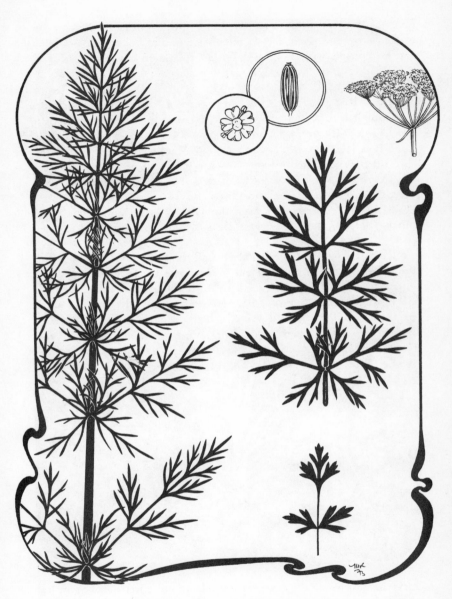

CARAWAY: with variation of foliage, beginning with first leaf, lower right, slightly older above and on the left a mature leaf; also umbel, enlarged flower and dried seed.

CHERVIL: just before the flowering stalk shoots up to treble its height; leaf details and seed head, and enlarged leaf tip, flowering head and flower, two portions of a seed and whole seed.

Chervil

Umbelliferae

Anthriscus cerefolium

This is Garden Chervil, not the wild one which so enhances the countryside in spring. It is a small, delicate plant, but when flower heads appear the stalk will shoot up very quickly to three times the height, and the flower will be over, seeds ripe, and the whole plant dead before one has remembered that it is best to remove flowering heads as soon as they appear. The shape of the leaves is very similar to those of Hemlock (see p. 147). Chervil usually has a pale leaf which never grows as large as those on the smallest Hemlock. As soon as Chervil leaves form they spread sideways, whereas Hemlock shoots directly upwards like an elegant fern. Chervil flower heads are quite tiny, the whole umbel barely exceeding an inch in width. The flowers are white, the ovaries extending to push the petals away from the stalk as the seed develops. Flowers in May and June.

Habitat and Cultivation: Middle East, and northeast of the Mediterranean. Not wild in the British Isles or the U.S.A., but is sometimes found as an escape from gardens, growing in hedgerows and moist areas; naturalized from Pennsylvania to Quebec. Annual, but plants can survive most winters. Propagation is by seed at intervals during the summer months to provide continuing supply. Once Chervil is established it will self-sow. It prefers some shade and may turn reddish if too dry or sunny. It grows usually between nine inches and a foot high, before the flowering stalks appear.

Kitchen: One of the most delightful herbs, delicate and subtle. Chop or tear leaves, a handful or two at a time. Chervil was one of the old Pot Herbs. **Soups:** Use as a garnish, and as Chervil soup. **Salads:** Use in vegetable salads, especially potato and tomato. **Vegetables:** Use to flavour artichoke hearts, beans, beets, carrots, cauliflower, eggplant, peas, potatoes, spinach and tomatoes. **Meat:** Make herb butters for meat and fish; use in terrines; mix with sour cream poured on to pork or veal while cooking. Use in egg and lemon sauces for all. **Drinks:** Make tea from the leaves. **Winter:** Use the fresh herb, or dried or deep-frozen. **Other uses:** Cook with millet and haricot beans.

Pottage of Chervil the Dutch Way: Get ready a sufficient Quantity of good Broth, and put in it a Knuckle of Veal, cut in Pieces, the Bigness of an Egg; skim it, and take care it does not boil too much. Half an Hour before you serve it to Table, throw in some Forc'd-Meat Balls, not too fat, but of a good Consistence; droll them before-hand in Raspings of Bread; they must be no bigger than small Nuts. A Quarter of an Hour before you serve, put in a pretty deal of Chervil mix'd and chopp'd very fine, together with a Handful of Flour, there must be a great deal; for a large Soop a good Plate full is requisite. When your Chervil is in, keep it always stirring till you are ready to serve, which must be without Bread.

Coriander

Umbelliferae

Coriandrum sativum

Coriander is of delicate growth, with a bewildering progression of leaf shapes, first broad and roundish, finally mere tracery. Bracts under the main umbel are sometimes absent, and can be either pronged or un-cut. Flowers are variable in colour from palest lilac and pink to white. The central heads of the umbels have small tightly arranged petals, edged with darker colour, but some of the outer petals on the outer flowers extend till the whole looks like a group of small pale butterflies at a picnic. It flowers in June and July.

Habitat and Cultivation: Southern Europe, in fields, waste places and river-sides. It is not found wild in the British Isles, but is well settled in parts of the U.S.A., particularly towards the south. Annual. Propagate by seed in a sunny bed in spring, and at later intervals to ensure continuous fresh leaves. Approximately eighteen inches high but less wide.

Kitchen: Young leaves are used, and the seeds, which have a mildly spicy flavour, remind me of pomanders, with the aroma of oranges and cloves. This flavour increases during storage, but diminishes quickly once ground. Like most spices used in curry, the aroma increases if the seed is ground and slightly roasted for a few minutes before using. Coriander is a principal Eastern herb, used mainly in curries, chutneys and pickles. It has a much wider variety of uses, and just a few seeds can transform a dish, though too many may spoil it (see p. 119). **Soups:** Use ground seed, and leaves as a garnish. **Salads:** In green salads or others use torn leaves or seeds, fresh or dried, particularly if olives are included. **Vegetables:** Cook seeds, whole or ground, or some leaves, with cauliflower, brussels sprouts, beets, fennel, leeks, potatoes. **Meat:** Use seed, whole or ground, with beef, fish, lamb, liver (particularly with apples, onions and wine), pork, veal. Use in casseroles, curries, and spiced dishes, sauces and sausages (see p. 15). **Cheese:** Use in cream and cottage cheeses. **Drinks:** Make a tea from the seeds, which can mix with others, e.g., Fennel. **Winter:** Use seeds or deep-frozen leaves, or those stored in oil. **Other uses:** Use ground in omelettes, whole in soufflés, especially those made with cheese and orange (see p. 80). Cook with rice, seed with chick peas and leaves with red kidney beans. Use seed whole or crushed in and on bread, cakes and jellies.

Beef-Steaks Rolled: Take three or four large Beef-Steaks, and flat them with a Cleaver: Make a Farce with the Flesh of a Capon, some of a Fillet of Veal, and some Gamon of Bacon, both Fat and Lean; add to this the Fat of a Loin of Veal, Sweetbreads, young Onions, Parsley, Mushrooms, and Truffles, the Yolks of four Eggs, with a little Cream; season all these with Spice and Herbs, and hash them, then strew them on your Slices of Beef, and roll it up very handsomely, that they may be firm, and of a good Size; then let them stew a good while. When they are enough, take them up, and drain away the Fat very well, then slit them in two, and lay them in a Dish, the cut Sides uppermost. You may put to them a Ragoo, or a good Cullis, as you please (see pp. 63 and 83).

CORIANDER: shows leaf changes with flowering head and enlarged flower with some stamens dropped; also the seed, smooth side fresh, wrinkled side dried.

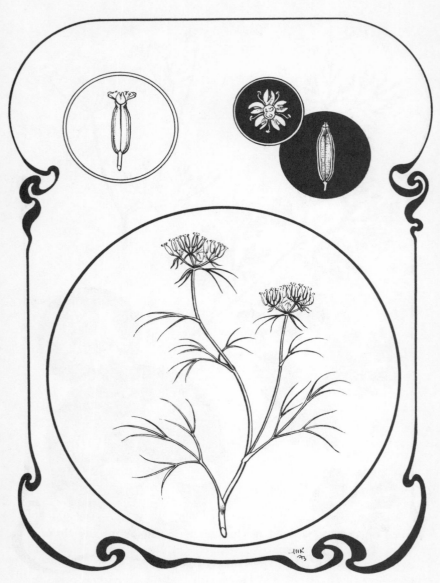

CUMIN: showing almost the whole plant, with enlarged fresh seed with petals still attached, enlarged flower and dried seed, also enlarged.

Cumin

Cuminum cyminum

Umbelliferae

Cumin is the merest wisp of a plant, slender weak stems barely support the fragile leaves, the lower of which are stalked, the upper not so. The pale pink flowers have turned-back tips, and show in June and July.

Habitat and Cultivation: Mediterranean, Middle East, India. Not wild in the British Isles or the U.S.A. Annual. Propagation is by seed into a sunny spot where larger plants will not crowd it. The small weak plant may grow approximately nine inches high.

Kitchen: The seeds are used, either ground or whole. Ground Cumin may be sold as Ground Jeera, which is a name used for several spices, so check that it actually is Cumin. The seed has a haunting flavour, and is essential in some Asian and Mexican dishes. **Soups:** Use sprinkled ground Cumin in soups, especially one based on potatoes cooked in chicken stock and mashed to thicken the liquid. Add at least half a teaspoon of ground Cumin, and increase quantity to taste. Add sour cream, seasoning, Chervil and/or Parsley. **Salads:** It combines well with mayonnaise, when ground; or use whole in green or potato salads and coleslaw. **Vegetables:** Sprinkle seeds into dishes of cabbage, carrots, cauliflower, eggplant, leeks, parsnips, green peppers, mashed potatoes and tomatoes. **Meat:** Sprinkle powder on roasting meat and kebabs, beef, chicken, lamb, mince, and pork. An orange sauce compliments these. It is also used in curry powders, chutneys, chillies and pickles. **Cheese:** Mix seeds into cream and cottage cheeses. **Winter:** Use seeds. **Other uses:** Cook with rice, or in rye bread. Use powder in Tahini paste to eat with breads, especially pitta bread.

Pheasants with Olives: Take as many Pheasants as you think will make up your Dish, pick, singe, and draw them clean; but don't cut the lowest Part of the Belly, or Vent. Take off the Galls from your Livers, and cut these small, with some Parsley, green Onions, Champignons, sweet Herbs, fine Spice, Pepper, Salt, scraped Bacon, and a Bit of Butter, and put all this into the Belly of your Pheasants, and thrust the Rump into the lower Part of the Belly, or Vent, to prevent your Forced-meat from coming out; blanch them in a Stew-pan, with Butter, Parsley, green Onions, Salt, Basil, all in Branches; put your Pheasants on the Spit, wrapp'd up in Slices of Bacon, and Paper ty'd round. Take some Olives, take out their Stones, blanch them in hot Water; they being blanch'd, put them in a Stew-pan, with Cullis, Essence of Ham and Gravy; put them a boiling, skimming the Fat well off; see that all together be relishing: Your Pheasants being roasted, draw them off, and take off the Slices of Bacon; dish them up, put your Olives over them, and serve them hot for an Entry for second Course. (For Cullis, see p. 63.)

Dill   *Umbelliferae*
Anethum graveolens

Dill usually has a single upright stalk, and is inclined, like other annual umbellifers, to gallop into flower and then die. First leaves are
finely divided, and later leaves become delicate wisps. Yellow
flowers are carried in flattish umbels in July and August.

Habitat and Cultivation: Mediterranean, southern Russia, in hedgerows and waste places. Not wild in the British Isles, but found
over most of the U.S.A. and Canada. Annual. Propagate by seed in
spring and at intervals later to ensure supply, planting into a sunny
place away from wind. Grow away from Fennel, as the two will
cross-pollinate and subsequent plants will probably not have the familiar flavours. Dill can grow to three feet high, and half as wide.

Kitchen: Use leaves, whole, chopped or torn, and seeds. Useful not
only for its flavour, but because it helps digestion and relieves
flatulence. Dill should be added to a dish just before completion of
cooking, as the flavour may diminish otherwise. **Soups:** Use in vegetable. **Salads:** Leaves as well as flowering heads or seeds can go into
most salads, but especially coleslaw, cucumber and sauerkraut, and
also in yoghurt and sour cream. **Vegetables:** Use leaves and/or
seeds with beans, beets, cabbage, carrots, cauliflower, celery, mush-

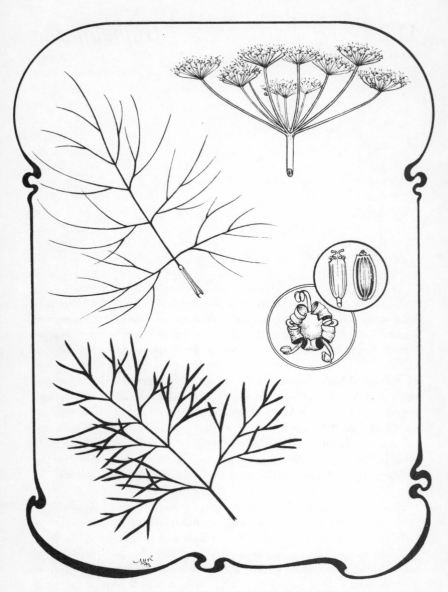

DILL: showing slight change in leaves, top one being mature: also umbel, and enlarged flower with some stamens still folded, side view of a fresh seed and front view of a dried seed.

rooms, parsnips, peas, potatoes and spinach. **Meat:** Use with beef, chicken, duck, fish, kidney, lamb, pork, veal, roasts, casseroles and in sauces for same. **Cheese:** Use in cream and cottage cheeses. **Drinks:** Make tea with seeds. **Winter:** Use seeds. **Other uses:** Sprinkle into omelettes, and apple pies. Cook with barley and rice, and in and on breads.

To Marinate Soals: Let large Soals be well washed, skin'd, and dry'd; that done, beat them with a Rolling-pin, and dip them on both Sides in the Yolks of Eggs temper'd with Flour; Then putting your Fish into a Fry-pan, with as much Florence Oil as will cover them, fry them till they are brown, and come to a bright yellow Colour, or fry them in clarified Butter: At that Instant take them up, drain them on a Plate, and set them by to cool. For the Pickle take White Wine Vinegar well boiled with Salt, Pepper, Nutmeg, Cloves, and Mace: It is requisite to turn the Liquor into a broad earthen Pan, that the Fish may lie at full Length; and the Dish is to be garnished with Flowers, Fennel, Dill, and Lemon-peel.

To Dress a Leg of Mutton with Cucumbers: First marinate your Cucumbers, then toss them up, and make a Ragoo of them, take some Bacon, and brown a little Flour; put to it some good Gravy, a Drop of Vinegar, and a Bundle of savoury Herbs, and season all well. Roast the Leg of Mutton, and serve it up with this Ragoo. In the like Manner you may make a Ragoo of Succory, but take care the Succory turn not black in the Dressing. (Succory: wild endive, or chicory.)

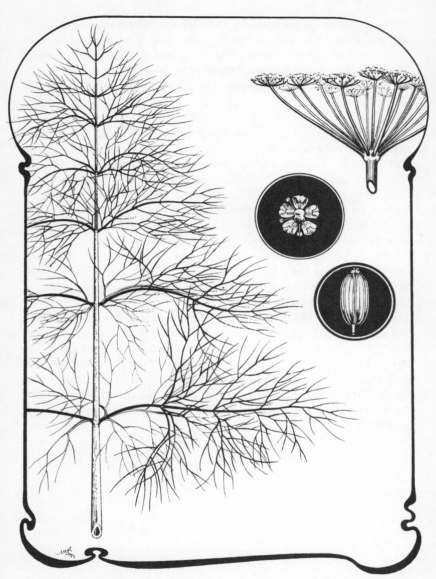

FENNEL: showing the much divided leaf of a mature plant of Sweet Fennel, also an umbel, enlarged flower with some stamens dropped, and a drying seed. Fresh seed is less corrugated.

Fennel   *Umbelliferae*

Foeniculum vulgare, Sweet Fennel
Foeniculum dulce, Florence Fennel

Sweet Fennel in its second and subsequent years sends up several stalks, branched and carrying masses of delicate foliage, and eventually flattish umbels of yellow flowers from July to September. The whole effect in full flower is misty and golden.

Habitat and Cultivation: Temperate Europe, Mediterranean, and the U.S.A., where it has become widely spread. Perennial, dies down in winter. Propagate by seed in spring, in a warm position away from Dill, to avoid cross-pollination and the consequences that new plants will be a mixture of flavour, and not as good as the originals. It is best to pull off flower heads if the bush is to remain feathery and supply a quantity of leaves.

FLORENCE FENNEL is very similar to Sweet Fennel, but has swollen leaf bases which form a beautiful shape, looking as if celery had decided to try to become an onion. The foliage can be used much as Sweet Fennel.

Habitat and Cultivation: Propagate by seed; the plant is an annual, but late-sown seedlings may survive the winter and flower early next year. This variety needs to be kept moist.

Kitchen: Use the leaves, whole or chopped, from both varieties; seeds of Sweet Fennel, and swollen leaf bases of Florence Fennel, either whole or sliced, cooked or raw. Fennel aids digestion. **Soups:** Use seeds and leaves, or make a soup from finely chopped Florence Fennel. **Salads:** Use seeds, flower heads and leaves in all kinds. Young stems of Sweet Fennel can be eaten raw with a dressing, as can Florence Fennel. These can also be cooked, or partly cooked to soften them. These stems, chopped and mixed with walnuts and apple chunks in mayonnaise are delicious. **Vegetables:** Cook leaves and seeds with beans, beets, brussels sprouts, cabbage, cauliflower, mushrooms, peas, tomatoes. Use whole Fennel shoots or bases served with cheese or egg and lemon sauce. **Meat:** Use leaves as a bed for fish, or scatter seeds on top. A good snack is made from cod steaks and leeks, cooked in butter with Fennel seed sprinkled about, and mixed with leaves, then the whole covered in grated cheese and grilled. Leaves and seeds go well with pork and veal, and in terrines and pâtés (see p. 117). **Cheese:** Use seeds and leaves in cream and cottage cheeses. **Drinks:** Make a tea from the seeds, crushed or whole, or use seeds mixed with other herb teas. One small teaspoon to each cup is a very pleasant drink, with orange peel added. The tea is good for flatulence and can be mixed with Coriander, Dill and Anise. **Winter:** Use seeds. **Other uses:** In breads and cakes, use whole seeds, or sprinkle ground Fennel on top. Cook seeds and leaves with rice, and seeds with lentils. Florence Fennel goes well with walnuts.

Lovage

Levisticum officinale

Umbelliferae

Lovage can be described as being vaguely like celery at first glance, but has such strangely irregular, torn-looking leaflets that there should be no confusion. These vary somewhat in size, the plant reaching sometimes about five feet in height, and are firm, flat and slightly thick, with simple veining. Some leaves do not have pronged leaflets at the tip, and in these cases the simple irregular shapes are echoed in other leaflets down the stem. Yellow flowers appear in July and August, with petals hardly opening, and the large centres dominant, with bright oily flecks on their surfaces.

Habitat and Cultivation: Mountainous areas of the Mediterranean, in sunny places and good, moist soil. It is not wild in the British Isles, but has escaped into parts of the U.S.A., which also has two related species, including *Ligusticum Scoticum,* a plant sometimes found in Scotland. In the U.S.A. found especially from Pennsylvania to Virginia. Perennial, dies down in winter. Propagate by fresh seed preferably in late summer, when seed is ripe, or by root division, in a sunny moist place with good soil, well drained. Lovage will grow approximately three to five feet high, or more, and about half as wide, and may take three or four years to mature.

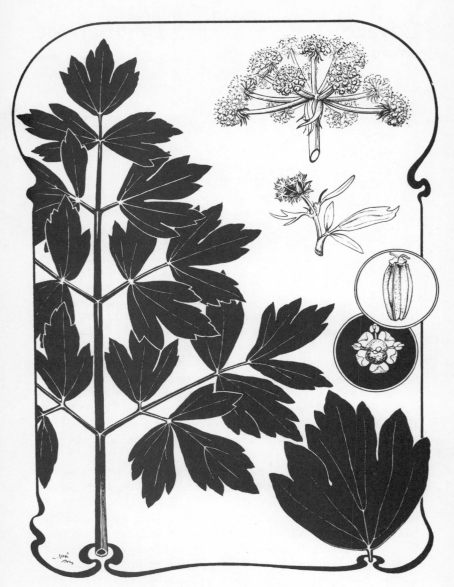

LOVAGE: part of a mature leaf, and the end leaflet from a larger leaf. Also opened and unopened umbels, one showing how each stalk has its own **bract**; and enlarged flower with some stamens dropped, and a fresh seed.

Kitchen: Leaves, seeds, young stems and roots are used; it is an old Pot Herb. **Soups:** Use chopped leaves in all kinds, or best of all soups—Lovage itself. Cook two large finely chopped onions in butter till golden, add two large handfuls of chopped Lovage, and when softened, add flour to thicken, pour in hot chicken stock and stir till smooth. Just before serving add lemon juice or sour cream and seasoning. **Salads:** Scattered seeds, leaves, chopped or torn, can be added to all kinds, particularly tomato and potato, or used in dressings. **Vegetables:** Leaves and stems can be cooked and served with plain or herb butter, or in a sauce made with cheese. Chopped leaves can be used to flavour other vegetables. Roots can be eaten either steamed or boiled, and were frequently used this way in the past. **Meat:** Use chopped leaves in casseroles and sauces. Whole seeds can be used as a garnish. **Drinks:** Make tea from the leaves. **Winter:** Leaves can be deep-frozen or dried. Seeds are available. **Other uses:** Candied stems can be prepared as Angelica (see p. 115). Lovage can be used in omelettes, and bread and biscuits.

To Make Meagre Broth for Soop with Herbs: Set on a Kettle of Water, put in two or three Crusts of Bread, and all Sorts of Herbs, season it with Salt; put in Butter, and a Bunch of sweet Herbs; boil it for an Hour and Half, then strain it through a Sieve or Napkin. This will serve to make Lettuce Soop, Artichoak Soop, Asparagus Soop, Succory Soop, and Soop de santé with Herbs.

SWEET CICELY: showing part of a leaf with the white hairs on the stem, a seed (not enlarged, they are very big), an enlarged flower whose stamens have dropped, and an umbel.

Sweet Cicely *Umbelliferae*
Myrrhis odorata

Sweet Cicely is a bushy, lacy plant, hairy everywhere except, apparently, the upper surface of the leaves; and exuding a sweet perfume. The leaves spread sideways as soon as they appear, and the white hairs underneath give a misty look. Umbels of white flowers with turned-back tips appear in May.

Habitat and Cultivation: Northern Europe, British Isles, not wild in the U.S.A., where the name applies to other umbelliferae. Hedgerows and ditches, partially shaded in damp waste ground. Perennial, dies down in winter. Propagate by seed, or root division in spring. Grows approximately two to four feet high and at least as wide.

Kitchen: Leaves, torn into salads; seeds, chopped; and peeled roots. **Salads:** Use raw leaves with fruit and vegetable salads. Roots can be boiled or steamed and served cold with a dressing. **Vegetables:** The leaves are cooked as spinach, and the roots cooked and served hot with a creamy sauce, with Coriander or other herbs. **Drinks:** Make tea from the leaves. **Winter:** Use deep-frozen leaves, and seeds. **Other uses:** As this is a sweet-flavoured herb, it reduces the tartness of some fruit dishes, and means that less sugar is needed in cooking gooseberries and rhubarb. Leaves and chopped seeds can be mixed into whipped cream.

To Make an Egg as Big as Twenty: Part the Yolks from the Whites of Twenty Eggs, strain the Yolks by themselves, and the Whites by themselves, boil the Yolks in a Bladder, in the form either of an Egg or Ball; when they are boiled hard, put the Ball of Yolks into another Bladder, and the Whites round about it, and bind it up oval or round, and boil it. These Eggs are used in grand Sallads.

If you please, you may add to the Yolks of Eggs Ambergreese, grated Biscuits, candy'd Pistachoes and Sugar; and to the Whites, Musk, Almond-paste, beaten Ginger, and the Juice of Oranges, and serve them up with Butter, Almond-milk, Sugar, and the Juice of Orange.

Pigeons Boiled with Rice: Take six Pigeons, stuff their Bellies with Parsley, Pepper and Salt roll'd in a very little Piece of Butter; put them into a Quart of Mutton-Broth, with a little beaten Mace, a Bundle of sweet Herbs, and an Onion; cover them close, and let them boil a full Quarter of an Hour; then take out the Onion and sweet Herbs, and take a good Piece of Butter rolled in Flour; put it in, and give it a Shake, season it with Salt, if it wants it; then have ready Half a Pound of Rice boiled tender in Milk; when it begins to be thick (but take great Care it don't burnt too) take the Yolks of two or three Eggs, beat up with two or three Spoonfulls of Cream and a little Nutmeg; stir it together till it is quite thick; then take up the Pigeons, and lay them in a Dish; pour the Gravy to the Rice; stir all together, and pour over the Pigeons. Garnish with hard Eggs cut into Quarters.

Poisonous Umbelliferae

There are several of these plants; too many to be illustrated, but the most dangerous in relation to the other herbs drawn are Hemlock and Fool's Parsley. All the rest grow in or near water, and *any* umbellifers so doing are simply best left alone. Hemlock is quite distinctive once seen because of its fine structure and brightly shiny leaves, slightly paler on the underside. The mature plant is, in the main, darkly ferny, with the foliage towards the flowering heads becoming paler, almost yellow, cascading upper leaves falling away under the misty umbels. It is always graceful even when a few inches high, stretching upwards, rather than spreading sideways like Chervil. The spattering of red on the stems may not appear till they are already several inches high and quite dangerous, and the much mentioned odours not always apparent while the plant remains undamaged. When it flowers in its second year the umbels are rounded and delicate, and the most valuable distinctive feature appears in the upper bracts. (See below.) The green fruits are at first two softly rounded shapes apparently pressed together, but the identifying ridges do not appear (in common with other umbelliferae) until the fruit is drying out. Anise and Coriander have been confused with Hemlock fruit, but Coriander, at least, is really quite round like a ball, with no evidence of wrinkles or segments while fo-

FOOL'S PARSLEY: showing a young leaf, contrasted with finer upper leaves under the umbel. Enlarged fresh seeds and flowers without stamens, and folded umbel before flowering; leaf, and a large seed head.

liage remains on the plant. Fool's Parsley forms flower heads very early, and the long bracts are visible tailing below the upper stalks of the umbel. Like Hemlock, these bracts appear on one side only. Both are illustrated.

HEMLOCK *Conium maculatum*

Biennial, stem smooth, covered with a soft bloom as are grapes. It is hollow and hairless; red flecked and blotched, two to eight feet high. Leaves are two to three pinnate, sharply cut; the lower as much as two feet long, the upper only a few inches. Lower bracts are linear, *the upper on one side only.* Flowers white, responsible for the "mousy smell" associated with hemlock (broken stems can smell awful, but I would not call their smell mousy) ; in late June, July, August. Fruit in rounded segments, developing five wavy ridges on each carpel as it ripens. Common. In Europe, temperate Asia, N. Africa, the British Isles, N. and S.—in both of which it has run wild over large areas—America and Canada. *On banks, hedgerows, waste places and beside streams.*

FOOL'S PARSLEY (Lesser Hemlock) *Aethusa cynapium*

Stems erect, hairless, hollow, ribbed; up to eighteen inches high. Leaves two to three pinnate, smooth. Lower bracts absent, upper a few only, very long and narrow, *and on the outer side only.* Flowers white, in July and August. Fruit oval with swollen ridges shrinking to three main ridges and two wings to each carpel, when dried. Common in much of the British Isles and the northeastern and middle United States. Found in *gardens and arable areas.*

COWBANE (Water Hemlock) *Cicuta virosa*

Stem stout, hairless, hollow, one to four feet high. Roots tuberous. Leaves two to three pinnate, with serrated leaflets. Lower bracts absent, upper many and strap-shaped. Flowers white, in July and August. Fruits round; when dried, five rounded ridges to each carpel. *Ponds and ditches,* in a few scattered places in the British Isles and the U.S.A.

HEMLOCK WATER DROPWORT *Oenanthe crocata*

Stem stout, hairless, usually hollow, ribbed, one to four feet high. Roots clustered, tuberous. Leaves two to three pinnate, glossy and greyish. Bracts small and thin, lower sometimes absent. Flowers white, in July and August. Fruit cylindrical, five ridges appearing on each carpel as it dries. *In watery places* in parts of the British Isles. Fine-leaved water dropwort (*Oenanthe aquatica*) can be found in the U.S.A., but I am not sure about the other Dropworts.

FINE-LEAVED WATER DROPWORT *Oenanthe aquatica;* ponds and ditches.

TUBULAR WATER DROPWORT *Oenanthe fistulosa;* in or near water.

PARSLEY WATER DROPWORT *Oenanthe lachenalii;* salt water marshes.

SULPHURWORT *Oenanthe siliafolia;* freshwater marshes.

HEMLOCK: showing whole plant when young, with the seed, half fresh, half dried; flower, first shoot of the new plant; one-sided bracts, on the margin the smaller mature leaf from below the flowers, also an umbel and a leaf.

Umbelliferae to be regarded with care

Other umbelliferae may in some cases be poisonous, possibly if taken in large quantities, but there is as yet insufficient authenticated evidence to list them as dangerous. It is worth remembering that several of our favourite vegetables are safe to eat because we now know what parts of the plants we should not eat; not to mention the dozens lurking in our gardens and which are treated so fondly by those who grow them. I would think that it was unwise to go browsing amongst the wild plants without knowledge, as it is likely to lead to unplanned effects, and not necessarily very nice ones.

Angelica, Caraway, Fennel and Sweet Cicely are the only umbelliferous herbs mentioned in this book which are likely to be found wild, so it is these which must be distinguished. As Garden Angelica is preferable to the wild variety, I would eat it only from a known plant. Caraway and Fennel could possibly be mistaken by beginners for the poisonous and feathery Oenanthe plants which grow in damp areas, so I would make sure that one is quite familiar with these two before attempting to sample them in the wild. Finally, Sweet Cicely is a native plant and may be considered similar to Cow Parsley. Both are almost covered with hairs, and in almost the same way (i.e., not apparently on the upper surfaces of the leaves). For comparison, see below, and pages 140–41 and 150; the seeds when showing will be the decisive parts, those of Sweet Cicely being very large and distinctive, even when green.

I have drawn only two plants in this section, as they seem most likely to be confusing; they have a half skull each, but must not be considered to be nearly as dangerous as those with full skulls, which are absolutely poisonous. I will just repeat my remark about avoiding *all* umbelliferous plants from damp areas, and couple it with another, which is that from my research I would think that those plants with very hairy stems should also be left alone. One of them, Giant Hogweed, will not be enticing as a meal and may well give some people nasty rashes; the rest may be quite safe, but they are definitely unlikely to be a joy to the palate.

COW PARSLEY *Anthriscus sylvestris*

The earliest white flowering umbellifer of spring, in lacy drifts everywhere. Stems almost hairless, hollow, ribbed, sometimes the whole plant is purplish; growing from eighteen inches to four feet high. Leaves are two to three pinnate, hairy underneath. Lower bracts usually absent, upper small, pointed. Flowers white, from April to June. Fruit is elongated, hairless, five slight ribs on each carpel when dried. *Common* in the British Isles, but found only in some parts of the U.S.A.

BUR CHERVIL *Anthriscus caucalis*

Stems are slender, almost hairless, hollow and ribbed; from a few inches to two feet high. Leaves are two to three pinnate, very finely cut. Lower bracts usually absent, upper small. Flowers white, in May, June. Fruit roundish, with a small peak, and covered with hooked spines. Found in parts of the British Isles, but it may not grow in the U.S.A. It likes disturbed ground and sandy waste places near the sea.

COW PARSLEY.

BUR CHERVIL.

Kitchen Summary

Beef: basil, bay, caraway, coriander, cumin, dill, hyssop, marigold, marjoram, mint, rosemary, sage, savories, tarragon, thyme.

Bread and Cakes: anise, caraway, coriander, cumin, dill, fennel, lovage, marigold, marjoram, rosemary.

Cheese: borage, basil, bergamot, caraway, chives, coriander, cumin, dill, fennel, lemon balm, marigold, marjoram, mint, parsley, rosemary, sage, salad burnet, savories.

Chicken: basil, bay, caraway, coriander, cumin, dill, lemon balm, marigold, marjoram, mint, rosemary, sage, savories, tarragon, thyme.

Drinks: angelica, anise, basil, bergamot, borage, caraway, catmint, chamomile, chervil, chickweed, comfrey, coriander, dandelion, dill, elder, fennel, hyssop, lemon balm, lovage, marigold, mint, rosemary, roses, sage, savories, stinging nettles, sweet cicely, thyme, violets.

Duck: dill, hyssop, mint, rosemary, sage, savories, tarragon.

Eel: basil, hyssop, mint, rosemary, sage, savories, thyme.

Eggs: anise, basil, chervil, chives, coriander, cumin, dill, lemon balm, lovage, marjoram, mint, parsley, rosemary, sage, savories, tarragon, thyme.

Fish: anise, basil, caraway, chives, coriander, dill, fennel, hyssop, lemon balm, marigold, marjoram, mint, parsley, rosemary, sage, savories, tarragon, thyme.

Fritters: borage, comfrey, elder.

Fruit: caraway, dill, hyssop (pies), lemon balm.

Game: bay, hyssop, marigold.

Goose: sage.

Grain: basil, caraway, chervil, chives, coriander, cumin, dill, fennel, hyssop, marigold, marjoram, rosemary, savories, tarragon, thyme.

Hare: bay, sage, tarragon.

Jams and Jellies: borage, elder, lemon balm, roses, violets.

Kidneys: dill, hyssop.

Lamb: basil, bay, caraway, coriander, cumin, dill, hyssop, lemon balm, marjoram, mint, rosemary, sage, savories, thyme.

Liver: basil, coriander, sage, tarragon.

Nuts: caraway, fennel, marjoram, sage, thyme.

Pasta: basil, bay, marjoram, rosemary, thyme.

Pâtés: basil, fennel, marjoram, rosemary, sage, savories, tarragon, thyme.

Pork: anise, basil, bergamot, chervil, coriander, cumin, dill, fennel, hyssop, lemon balm, marjoram, mint, rosemary, sage, savories, tarragon, thyme.

Potted Meats: bay, chives, rosemary, sage, savories, tarragon.

Puddings: elder, sweet cicely.

Pulses: basil, chervil, coriander, fennel, hyssop, marjoram, rosemary, sage, savories, tarragon, thyme.

Rabbit: marjoram, sage, savories, tarragon.

Salads: anise, basil, bergamot, borage, caraway, catmint, chervil, chickweed, chives, comfrey, coriander, cumin, dandelion, dill, elder, hyssop, lemon balm, lovage, marigold, marjoram, mint, parsley, rosemary, roses, salad burnet, savories, sweet cicely, tarragon, thyme, violets.

Shellfish: rosemary, thyme.

Soups: anise, basil, borage, caraway, chervil, chickweed, chives, coriander, cumin, dill, fennel, hyssop, lemon balm, lovage, marigold, marjoram, mint, parsley, rosemary, roses, sage, salad burnet, stinging nettles, savories, tarragon, thyme.

Terrines: basil, fennel, marjoram, rosemary, sage, savories, tarragon, thyme.

Turkey: sage, savories, thyme.

Veal: anise, basil, bergamot, chervil, coriander, dill, lemon balm, marjoram, rosemary, sage, savories, tarragon, thyme.

Vegetables: basil, bay, borage, caraway, chervil, chickweed, chives, comfrey, coriander, cumin, dandelion, dill, fennel, lovage, marjoram, mint, parsley, rosemary, sage, stinging nettles, savories, sweet cicely, tarragon, thyme.

Venison: bay, sage.

Vinegar: anise, basil, caraway, chervil, coriander, cumin, dill, elder, fennel, hyssop, lemon balm, lovage, marjoram, mint, rosemary, roses, salad burnet, savories, sweet cicely, tarragon, thyme.

Winter: *Fresh herbs,* chervil, chickweed, dandelion, hyssop, rosemary, sage, salad burnet, thyme, winter savory; *under cloches,* mint, marjoram, parsley. *Dried seeds,* anise, caraway, coriander, cumin, dill, fennel, lovage, rose hips.

References, Further Reading

No list of this kind can be complete, so I am mentioning those which I would consider most likely to be of interest. The majority are still in print; the others will only be obtainable from public libraries or second-hand bookshops.

For visual reference the older books generally have more useful drawings than the more modern; they are in the main elegant, well printed and accurate. *The Wild Flower Guide* by Edgar T. Wherry includes a section on "introduced" plants. Several of the books mentioned will be too botanical for the beginner, but can be very important reference. My list may lean heavily towards the European flora, for which I must apologise. I have left them in for the reason that they could be very useful for anyone hoping to venture into the subject while they are in Europe.

Arber, Agnes. *Herbals*. Cambridge University Press, 1912.

Botanical Society of the British Isles. *Atlas of the British Flora*. Nelson, 1962.

British Herbal Medicine Association. *British Herbal Pharmacopoeia*. 1972.

Britton, Nathaniel Lord, and Brown, H. Addison. *Illustrated Flora of the Northern States and Canada and the British Possessions*. New York: Charles Scribner's Sons, 1897.

Brownlow, Margaret. *Herbs and the Fragrant Garden*. Darton, Longman and Todd, 1963.

Butcher, R. W. *A New Illustrated British Flora* (2 vols.). L. Hill, 1961.

Clapham, A. R., Tutin, T. G., and Warburg, E. F. *Flora of the British Isles,* and *Excursion Flora of the British Isles*. Cambridge University Press (black and white illustrations by S. Roles, in separate volumes).

Clarkson, Rosetta, E. *Herbs, Their Culture and Uses*. New York: Macmillan, 1942.

———— *The Golden Age of Herbs and Herbalists*. New York: Dover Publications, 1972. (First published in 1940 as *Green Enchantment: The Magic Spell of Gardens*.)

Culpeper, Nicholas. *The Complete Herbal,* 1653.

Dana, Mrs. William Starr. *How to Know the Wild Flowers*. New York: Charles Scribner's Sons, 1900.

Genders, Roy. *Scented Wildflowers of Britain*. Collins, 1971.

Gerard, John. *The Herbal,* 1597.

Gibbons, Euell. *Stalking the Wild Asparagus* and *Stalking the Healthful Herbs*. New York: David McKay Company, Inc., 1971, 1972.

Gleason, Henry A., and Conquist, A. *Manual of Vascular Plants of Northeastern U. S. and Adjacent Canada*. Princeton, N.J.: D. Van Nostrand Company, Inc., 1963.

Grieve, Maud. *A Modern Herbal* (2 vols.). Jonathon Cape, 1931, and New York: Hafner Publishing Company, 1971.

Hadfield, Miles. *Everyman's Wild Flowers and Trees*. London: Readers Union, J. M. Dent & Sons, 1957.

Hall, Dorothy. *The Book of Herbs*. Angus and Robertson, 1972.

Hatfield, Audrey Wynne. *Pleasures of Herbs*. London: Thorsons Publishers Ltd., 1972.

———— *How to Enjoy Your Weeds*. London: Frederick Muller, 1969.

Hemphill, Rosemary. *Herbs and Spices*. Harmondsworth, Eng.: Penguin, 1966.

Hutchinson, John. *British Wild Flowers* (2 vols.). Pelican, 1955.

Johns, Rev. C. A. *Flowers of the Field*. S.P.C.K., 1889

Keble, Martin, W. *The Concise British Flora in Colour*. London: Ebury Press, Michael Joseph, 1965.

Kingsbury, J. John M. *Deadly Harvest*. London: George Allen and Unwin Ltd., 1967 (also published in the U.S.A.).

Kreig, Margaret B. *Green Medicine, the Search for Plants that Heal*. London: George G. Harrap & Sons Ltd., 1965.

Law, Donald. *Herbs for Cooking and Healing*. Slough, Eng.: W. Foulsham and Co. Ltd., 1970.

———— *Herbal Teas for Health and Pleasure*. Health Science Press, 1970.

Levy, Juliette de Bairacli. *Herbal Handbook for Everyone*. London: Faber and Faber Ltd., 1966.

Loewenfeld, Claire. *Herb Gardening*. London: Faber and Faber Ltd., 1964.

———— and Back, Phillipa. *Herbs for Health and Cookery*. London: Pan, 1965.

Lovelock, Yann. *The Vegetable Book.* London: George Allen and Unwin Ltd., 1972.

Mabey, Richard. *Food for Free.* London: William Collins Sons & Co. Ltd., 1972.

Masefield, G. B., Wallis, M., Harrison, S. G., and Nicholson, B. E. *Oxford Book of Food Plants.* London: Oxford University Press, 1969.

McClintock, David. *Companion to Flowers.* G. Bell and Sons Ltd., 1966.

———— and Fitter, R. S. R. *The Pocket Guide to Wild Flowers.* London: William Collins Sons & Co. Ltd., 1971.

Macleod, Dawn. *A Book of Herbs.* London: Gerald Duckworth & Co. Ltd., 1968.

Minstry of Agriculture. *British Poisonous Plants.* H.M.S.O., Bulletin No. 161, 1954.

Mondenke, N. H. *American Wild Flowers.* Toronto/London: D. Van Nostrand, 1949.

North, Pamela. *Poisonous Plants and Fungi.* London: Blandford, 1967.

Platt, Rutherford. *This Green World.* New York: Dodd, Mead & Company, 1960.

Polunin, Oleg. *The Concise Flowers of Europe.* London: Oxford University Press, 1972.

Ranson, Florence. *British Herbs.* Harmondsworth, Eng.: Pelican, 1954.

Rohde, Eleanour Sinclair. *A Garden of Herbs.* New York: The Medici Society and Dover Publications, Inc. *The Old English Herbals.* Minerva Press, 1972 (first published 1922). *Vegetable Cultivation and Cookery.* New York: Medici Society, 1938.

Ross-Craig, Stella. *Drawings of British Plants.* London: G. Bell and Sons Ltd., 1947–74.

Saneki, Kay N. *Discovering Herbs.* Shire Publications, Tring, 1970.

Step, Edward. *Wayside and Woodland Blossoms.* London: Frederick Warne & Co. Ltd., 1963.

Stobart, Tom. *Herbs, Spices and Flavourings.* Newton Abbot, Eng.: David and Charles, 1970.

Sturtevant, E. Lewis (Ed., U. P. Hendrick). *Edible Plants of the World,* 1919. New York: Dover Publications, 1972.

Taylor, Norman. *A Guide to the Wild Flowers.* New York: Garden City Publishing Co. Inc., 1928.

Torrey, John, and Gray, Asa. *A Flora of North America* (facsimile of 1838–43 ed.). New York and London: Hafner Publishing Co., 1969.

University of the State of New York. *Wild Flowers of New York.* 1919.

Wherry, Edgar T. *Wild Flower Guide, Northeastern and Midland U.S.* Garden City, N.Y.: Doubleday & Company, Inc., 1948.